FISH DISHES

Clare Gordon-Smith

CHANCEL
PRESS

CONTENTS

First published in Great Britain in 1985

This edition published in 1994 by Chancellor Press
an imprint of Reed Consumer Books Limited
Michelin House, 81 Fulham Road, London SW3 6RB
and Auckland, Melbourne, Singapore and Toronto

Copyright © 1985 Reed International Books Limited

ISBN 1 85152 513 0

A CIP catalogue record for this book is available from the British Library

Produced by Mandarin Offset
Printed and bound in Hong Kong

INTRODUCTION

With today's emphasis on a healthy diet, what can be better than a natural fresh ingredient that can become a meal in minutes and is also extremely nutritious? Fish is one of the few foods that fits this description.

Take a small white fish, wash it, place a small knob of butter on it, place it under the grill and within minutes you have a ready-portioned meal, without the fuss of trimming or preparation.

Fish can be grilled, steamed, poached in a court bouillon, fried or filled with a tasty stuffing and baked in the oven. They can also take a great variety of sauces to complement their flavour and texture. Choose from the delicious freshly made sauces and savoury butters to bring out the best in your fish dishes.

There are many types of fish available, but don't let this put you off. Instead, welcome it as a wonderful opportunity to make the most of fish and use it to meet some of your dietary needs. Fish is an excellent source of protein, minerals and vitamins. With the wide variety of recipes to choose from, you should be able to please both family and friends at breakfast, lunch and dinner.

NOTES
Standard spoon measurements are used in all recipes.
1 tablespoon = one 15 ml spoon
1 teaspoon = one 5 ml spoon
All spoon measures are level.

Fresh herbs are used unless otherwise stated. If unobtainable substitute a bouquet garni of the equivalent dried herbs, or use dried herbs instead but halve the quantities stated.

Use freshly ground black pepper where pepper is specified.

Ovens should be preheated to the specified temperature.

For all recipes, quantities are given in both metric and imperial measures. Follow either set but not a mixture of both, because they are not interchangeable.

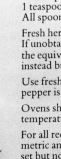

TYPES OF FISH

White fish, such as cod, plaice, hake, turbot, is so called because of its white flesh. It has only a small fat content, so be careful not to dry it out when cooking.

Oily fish such as mackerel, herring, sardines. This has a higher fat content than white fish and is often served with fruity sauces to counteract the fat.

Shellfish falls into two groups:
Jointed shells – crabs, prawns.
Hinged shells – oysters, mussels, clams, cockles.

Freshwater fish such as salmon, trout, carp. These come from lakes and streams.

CHOOSING AND BUYING FISH

Buying fresh fish is easy these days due to the increase in refrigerated equipment, both in transportation and in the fishmongers. Check for the following signs to make sure the fish you are buying is fresh.

- The overall colour should be bright and alive, with the skin shining.
- The eyes should appear bright and bulging with black pupils.
- The gills should be clean and bright red.
- If buying cutlets or steaks the flakes should be firm.
- Fresh fish should have a pleasant odour that you would not find offensive.

PREPARATION OF FISH FOR COOKING

Your fishmonger will be pleased to prepare the fish for you. Always ask for the waste items, such as skin and bones, to use for making fish stock for soups and sauces.

If, however, you do need to skin and fillet smaller fish, such as plaice or Dover sole, it is not difficult. Follow these simple instructions.

To fillet a fish: Place the fish on a board. Run a sharp knife along the centre bone. Scrape along the bones from the head end towards the tail until the fillet is released. Repeat on the other side. Now turn the fish over and remove the other 2 fillets in exactly the same way.

To skin a fillet: Place the fish fillet on a board, tail end towards you, flesh uppermost. Hold the tail firmly. With a sharp filleting knife, keeping the blade as close to the skin as possible, work your way down the fillet.

To skin a whole small fish (so that it can be cooked on the bone): Make a nick in the skin at the tail end, insert a finger and run it up the fish between the skin and the flesh. Ease the skin away from the flesh, pulling towards the head. Repeat this

process on the other side.

   If at any time the skin is too slippery to hold, dip your fingers in salt.

To scale a fish, such as red mullet: hold the fish at the tail. Use the back of a knife and scrape towards the head to remove the scales.

To gut a whole fish, such as herring: using a sharp knife, slit open the belly and ease out the guts. Rinse the fish inside and out under running cold water.

COOKING FISH

Fresh fish has a tender delicate flesh. For this reason, fish is cooked to develop its flavour rather than to tenderise it.

   Fish therefore needs careful, gentle cooking, over a moderate temperature for a short time. High heat and lengthy cooking times only toughen the flesh and destroy the flavour.

   The following methods are the most favourable to fish.

Poaching: Often used for large fish.

   Warm the liquid, such as fish stock, milk, water, wine, and add any flavouring, such as bouquet garni, lemon slices, herbs. Place the fish or fillet in the liquid and cook very gently for 10 to 15 minutes for fillets and 8 to 10 minutes per 500 g (1 lb) for whole fish; do not allow to boil.

Steaming: May be used for whole fish and fillets, but make sure they are well seasoned.

   Heat some water in a saucepan to simmering point. Place the fish on a buttered plate, cover with another plate, and place on top of the pan. Steam for about 10 minutes.

Grilling: A quick method of cooking fish. Useful for whole fish such as herring and kippers, and fillets such as plaice.

   Brush the fish with oil or dot with savoury butter (see page 92) to prevent it from drying. Cook for 5 to 10 minutes, turning the fish over halfway through cooking time.

   If grilling whole fish, leave their heads and tails on; this will keep them moist and juicy.

   If using fish which is thicker in parts, make diagonal slashes in the thickest parts to allow the heat to penetrate.

Baking: Suitable for whole fish, fillets and steaks.

   Place the fish in an ovenproof dish and pour in liquid such as fish stock, wine, milk, water. Add flavourings such as herbs, thinly chopped onion, carrots and celery, and sliced lemon.

   Cover with foil and bake in a preheated moderate oven, 180°C (350°F), Gas Mark 4, for 15 to 20 minutes. Remove from the cooking liquid with a fish slice; use the liquid in a sauce.

Braising: This can be done on the hob or in the oven.

Brown some chopped vegetables, eg celery, onion and carrot, in melted butter in a casserole dish. Cut the fish into large chunks or keep in steaks and add to the pan. Pour in about 1.25 litres (2¼ pints) water or stock and 150 ml (¼ pint) wine, cider or vinegar. Add salt and pepper to taste and herbs.

Cook in a preheated moderate oven, 180°C (350°F), Gas Mark 4, for 25 to 30 minutes, or on top of the stove for 20 minutes.

Shallow frying: Suitable for small whole fish, fillets and steaks.

Coat the fish in breadcrumbs, oatmeal, flour or a batter to protect the fish and prevent it from drying out.

Heat enough oil or butter in a large heavy-based frying pan to cover the base and give about 1-2.5 cm (½-1 inch) depth. Add the fish and cook over a moderate heat for 5 to 10 minutes on each side, depending on the thickness of the fish. Drain on kitchen paper.

Deep-frying: Similar to shallow-frying, except the fish is totally immersed in deep oil. Suitable for small whole fish, fillets, steaks and scampi.

Coat the fish as for shallow-frying. Fill a deep pan no more than half full with oil and heat to 180°C (350°F); if a thermometer is not available, drop a cube of day-old bread into the hot oil – if it browns in 60 seconds the oil is hot enough. If the oil is too hot, the coating will brown before the fish is cooked; if it's not hot enough, the coating will be heavy and soggy.

Lower the fish carefully into the hot oil, preferably in a frying basket, and cook for 4 to 8 minutes, depending on the size of the fish. Don't cook too many small pieces at once, e.g. scampi, or the temperature of the oil will be lowered and they will be soggy. Drain on kitchen paper.

TO TEST IF FISH IS COOKED

1. Insert a fork into the fleshiest part of the fish; the flesh will flake away if cooked.
2. The flesh loses its translucence and becomes opaque.
3. A milky curd appears on white fish when cooked.

COURT BOUILLON

A stock in which to braise or poach fish.

2 onions, sliced
3 carrots, sliced
2 celery sticks, sliced
2 lemon slices
25 g (1 oz) bunch of
   parsley
1 bay leaf
1 tablespoon salt
6 black peppercorns
15 g (½ oz) butter
600 ml (1 pint) dry white
   wine
1.2 litres (2 pints) water

Place all the ingredients in a pan, bring to the boil, then cover and simmer for 20 minutes. Allow to cool to blood heat before adding the fish.

Once the fish has been cooked, the stock can be strained and used as a basis for sauces for added flavour.
Makes 1.75 litres (3 pints)

FISH FUMET

A concentrated fish-flavoured stock. A good basis for fish soups.

bones and trimmings of
   2-3 fish, such as sole,
   salmon, cod or plaice
2 celery sticks, sliced
2 onions, sliced
1 carrot, sliced
1 bay leaf
1 teaspoon salt
2.5 litres (4½ pints)
   water
150 ml (¼ pint) dry
   white wine (optional)

Place all the ingredients in a large pan, bring to the boil, then simmer, uncovered, for 30 to 45 minutes, until reduced to 1.5 litres (2½ pints).

11

BREAKFASTS AND BRUNCHES

KEDGEREE

This delicious recipe was a traditional breakfast dish among the British in India.

350 g (12 oz) smoked cod fillet
175 g (6 oz) brown rice, cooked
1 egg, hard-boiled and chopped
½ teaspoon paprika
150 g (5 oz) natural yogurt
salt and pepper
25 g (1 oz) butter
lime or lemon wedges to garnish

Place the smoked cod on a plate over a saucepan of simmering water, cover and steam for 7 to 10 minutes, until it flakes when tested. Remove the skin and flake the flesh.

Mix the cod with the brown rice, chopped egg, paprika, yogurt, and salt and pepper to taste. Place in an ovenproof dish and dot with the butter.

Cook in a preheated moderate oven, 180°C (350°F), Gas Mark 4, for 30 minutes. Garnish with lime or lemon wedges to serve.
Serves 4

HAM AND HADDIE

350 g (12 oz) smoked
    haddock
40 g (1½ oz) unsalted
    butter
4 small thin slices
    gammon
parsley sprig to garnish

Divide the haddock into 4 portions
and poach in boiling water for
5 minutes. Drain well and remove
any skin and bones.

Melt the butter in a large frying
pan, add the gammon slices and fry
gently for 3 minutes.

Put a piece of haddock on top of
each slice of gammon in the pan,
cover and cook for 5 minutes.

Transfer to a warmed serving dish,
garnish with parsley and serve hot.
Serves 4
VARIATION: For an extra special treat,
pour 3 tablespoons double cream
over the fish and gammon and place
under a preheated hot grill for
2 minutes. Serve immediately.

HERRINGS IN OATMEAL

6 tablespoons medium
   oatmeal
salt and pepper
4 herrings, cleaned and cut
   into fillets
15 g (½ oz) butter
1 tablespoon oil
lemon wedges and parsley
   to garnish

Season the oatmeal with salt and
pepper and use to coat the herring
fillets. Melt the butter and oil in a
frying pan, add 2 fillets at a time and
fry for 4 to 5 minutes on each side,
until golden.

Garnish with lemon wedges and
parsley and serve hot.
Serves 4

CODDLED EGGS

50 g (2 oz) smoked
   salmon, cut into small
   pieces
4 eggs
salt and pepper
4 tablespoons double
   cream
chervil sprigs to garnish

Grease 4 ramekin dishes and divide
the smoked salmon between them.

Break an egg into each dish, on top
of the smoked salmon pieces. Season
with salt and pepper to taste and top
each dish with 1 tablespoon cream.

Place the dishes in a roasting pan
containing enough water to reach half
way up the ramekin dishes.

Cook in a preheated moderate
oven, 180°C (350°F), Gas Mark 4, for
10 to 15 minutes or until set. Garnish
with chervil and serve immediately.
Serves 4

KIPPERS WITH MARMALADE

1 pair of kippers
15 g (½ oz) unsalted
   butter
TO SERVE:
orange wedges
1 slice buttered brown
   bread
1 tablespoon orange
   marmalade

Remove the head and trim the tail of
the kippers with kitchen scissors.
Line a grill pan with foil. Place the
kippers on the foil, skin side
uppermost, and cook under a
preheated moderate grill for
1 minute. Turn the kippers over,
dot with the butter and grill for a
further 5 minutes, until sizzling.

Serve immediately, garnished with
orange wedges and accompanied by
the brown bread and marmalade.
Serves 1
NOTE: If you don't like the smell of
cooking kippers, try this method:
place them in a saucepan, cover with
boiling water and put on the lid.
Simmer for 5 minutes. Drain well.

KIPPER PÂTÉ

This is a good breakfast dish, as it can be made in advance and kept in the refrigerator for several days.

500 g (1 lb) frozen kipper
  fillets
65 g (2½ oz) unsalted
  butter
113 g (4 oz) cottage
  cheese
2 tablespoons lemon juice
pepper
TO GARNISH:
lemon and orange slices
chervil sprigs

Cook the kipper fillets according to packet instructions. Flake the fish slightly, then place in a food processor or electric blender with 25 g (1 oz) of the butter, the cheese, lemon juice, and pepper to taste. Work until smooth.

Divide the mixture between 4 ramekin dishes and smooth the surface. Melt the remaining butter and pour a little over each ramekin. Chill for at least 2 hours before serving.

Garnish with lemon and orange slices and chervil sprigs. Serve with hot wholewheat toast.
Serves 4 to 6

ARBROATH PANCAKES

BATTER:
125 g (4 oz) wholewheat
  flour
1 egg
300 ml (½ pint) milk
1 tablespoon sunflower oil
FILLING:
350 g (12 oz) tomatoes,
  chopped
4 spring onions, chopped
1 teaspoon clear honey
pepper
1 arbroath smokie,
  skinned and flaked
basil leaves to garnish

Place the flour in a bowl, add the egg and gradually beat in the milk until a smooth batter is formed.

Heat the oil in a 20 cm (8 inch) frying pan, pour in about 2 tablespoons of the batter and tilt the pan to coat the base evenly. Cook until the batter has set and the edges are golden brown. Turn the pancake over and cook for a further 20 seconds. Turn onto a warmed plate, cover with greaseproof paper and keep warm. Repeat with the remaining batter to make 6 pancakes.

To make the filling, place the tomatoes, spring onions, honey, and pepper to taste in a saucepan, bring to the boil, then simmer for 5 minutes. Stir in the smokie.

Divide the filling between the pancakes and fold up into triangles. Garnish with basil and serve immediately.
Serves 6

NEW ENGLAND CLAM CHOWDER

50 g (2 oz) butter
2 spring onions, chopped
40 g (1½ oz) plain flour
pinch of cayenne pepper
salt and pepper
600 ml (1 pint) fish stock
1 × 175 g (6 oz) can
   clams
125 g (4 oz) frozen
   peeled prawns, thawed
1 × 198 g (7 oz) can
   sweetcorn, drained
2 potatoes, cubed
142 ml (5 fl oz) soured
   cream
chopped parsley

Melt the butter in a pan, add the
spring onions and fry until softened.
Stir in the flour, cayenne, and salt and
pepper to taste and cook for 1 minute.
Gradually add the stock and bring to
the boil. Add the clams, prawns,
sweetcorn and potatoes and simmer
for 15 minutes, or until the potatoes
are soft but still hold their shape.

Stir in the soured cream. Sprinkle
with the parsley to serve.
Serves 4

17

HADDOCK AND MUSHROOM OMELET

25 g (1 oz) butter
125 g (4 oz) mushrooms,
    sliced
4 eggs, beaten
250 g (8 oz) smoked
    haddock, steamed and
    flaked (see Wholewheat
    Fish Burgers, below)

Melt the butter in a frying pan, add the mushrooms and fry gently for 2 to 3 minutes, until tender.

Add the egg and cook over a low heat for 3 to 4 minutes. When just beginning to set, add the flaked fish and cook for 1 minute. Fold the omelet in half and serve immediately.
Serves 2

HERRING ROES ON TOAST

500 g (1 lb) soft herring
    roes
2 tablespoons plain flour
salt and pepper
50 g (2 oz) unsalted
    butter
1 tablespoon anchovy
    essence
1 teaspoon lemon juice
2 drops Tabasco sauce
1/2 teaspoon paprika
2 slices wholewheat
    buttered toast to serve

Place the roes in a colander and pour over boiling water. Dry with kitchen paper. Season the flour with salt and pepper and use to coat the roes.

Melt the butter in a pan until foaming, add the roes and remaining ingredients and fry for about 3 to 5 minutes, until crisp and golden.

Cut the toast into triangles. Put the cooked roe on a warmed serving plate, surround with the toast and serve immediately.
Serves 2 to 4

WHOLEWHEAT FISH BURGERS

250 g (8 oz) smoked
    haddock
500 g (1 lb) potatoes,
    boiled and mashed
1 spring onion, chopped
salt and pepper
25 g (1 oz) butter
2 eggs, beaten
50 g (2 oz) wholewheat
    flour
125 g (4 oz) fresh
    wholewheat
    breadcrumbs
2 tablespoons oil

Place the haddock on a plate over a pan of boiling water, cover and steam for 10 to 15 minutes, until the fish flakes easily from the skin. Remove the skin and any bones; flake the fish.

Mix together the potato, fish, spring onion, and salt and pepper to taste. Add the butter and a little of the egg to bind the mixture together. Season the flour with salt and pepper. Shape the mixture into 8 burgers and coat with the seasoned flour. Dip in the beaten egg and coat with the breadcrumbs. Heat the oil in a frying pan, add the fish burgers and fry for 2 to 3 minutes on each side, until crisp and golden. Serve hot.
Makes 8

LUNCHES AND SUPPERS

PLAICE WITH SMOKED SALMON IN LEMON SAUCE

2 plaice, filleted and
   skinned
50 g (2 oz) smoked
   salmon, in 2 slices
250 g (8 oz) frozen
   chopped spinach,
   thawed
15 g (½ oz) butter
15 g (½ oz) plain flour
150 ml (¼ pint) milk
2 tablespoons lemon juice
salt and pepper
TO GARNISH:
lemon wedges
parsley sprigs

Take 2 plaice fillets and lay a piece of smoked salmon on top of each. Place the remaining fillets on top.

Place the spinach in a buttered ovenproof dish, large enough to hold the plaice side by side. Arrange the fish on top of the spinach.

Melt the butter in a pan, stir in the flour and cook for 1 minute. Gradually stir in the milk and bring to the boil. Stir in the lemon juice, and salt and pepper to taste. Pour over the fish.

Cook in a preheated moderate oven, 180°C (350°F), Gas Mark 4, for 10 to 15 minutes. Garnish with lemon wedges and parsley to serve.
Serves 2

RED MULLET WITH CHICORY

350 g (12 oz) chicory
salt and pepper
25 g (1 oz) unsalted
   butter
1 small onion, sliced
1 shallot, finely sliced
2 teaspoons lemon juice
salt and pepper
4 small red mullet, cleaned
   and scaled
TO GARNISH:
dill sprigs
lemon wedges

Blanch the chicory in boiling salted water for 5 minutes. Drain, then break off and slice the leaves.

Melt the butter in a pan, stir in the onion, shallot, chicory, lemon juice, and salt and pepper to taste. Cover and cook for 5 minutes.

Spoon into an ovenproof dish. Place the red mullet on top and sprinkle with salt and pepper. Cover with foil and cook in a preheated moderate oven, 180°C (350°F), Gas Mark 4, for 20 minutes or until cooked. Garnish with dill and lemon to serve.

Serves 4

VARIATION: Replace the chicory with sliced fennel.

TAGLIATELLE WITH SMOKED BUCKLING

250 g (8 oz) dried
   tagliatelle verdi
1 tablespoon sunflower oil
50 g (2 oz) mushrooms,
   sliced
250 g (8 oz) Boursin
   cheese
350 g (12 oz) smoked
   buckling, skinned,
   boned and flaked
1 tablespoon chopped
   parsley to garnish

Cook the tagliatelle according to packet directions.

Meanwhile, heat the oil in a large pan, add the mushrooms and sauté for 3 minutes. Add the cheese and heat gently until melted; be careful not to boil.

Drain the tagliatelle, add to the pan, then stir in the fish.

Garnish with the parsley and serve immediately.
Serves 4

CORNISH EEL

25 g (1 oz) butter
1 onion, chopped
500-750 g (1-1½ lb)
   conger eel, cut into
   slices
15 g (½ oz) plain flour
450 ml (¾ pint) dry cider
1 cooking apple, peeled,
   cored and sliced
2 cloves
salt and pepper
TO GARNISH:
mint or parsley sprigs
lemon slices

Melt the butter in a flameproof casserole, add the onion and fry until softened.

Add the eel pieces and brown lightly. Stir in the flour and cook for 2 minutes, stirring, then gradually pour in the cider, stirring. Add the apple, cloves, and salt and pepper to taste and bring to the boil. Cook in a preheated moderate oven, 180°C (350°F), Gas Mark 4, for 1 hour.

Garnish with mint or parsley and lemon and serve immediately.
Serves 4

CITRUS HALIBUT STEAK

grated rind and juice of 1
   orange, lemon and lime
1 halibut steak, cut in half
TO GARNISH:
2 orange, lemon and lime
   slices

Place 1 tablespoon of each grated rind and all the fruit juices in an ovenproof dish. Add the fish and baste well. Cover and chill for 12 hours, turning the steaks over after 6 hours.

Cover the dish with foil and cook in a preheated moderate oven, 180°C (350°F), Gas Mark 4, for 20 minutes.

Garnish each portion with an orange, lemon and lime slice and serve with mangetouts.
Serves 2

TANDOORI SOLE

½ teaspoon chilli powder
½ teaspoon turmeric
½ teaspoon ground
   coriander
½ teaspoon ground cumin
1 teaspoon ground ginger
½ teaspoon garam masala
¼ teaspoon salt
pepper
300 g (10 oz) natural
   yogurt
2 cloves garlic, crushed
2 drops of cochineal
2 lemon sole, skinned and
   filleted
TO GARNISH:
coriander leaves
lime wedges

Mix all the spices together, adding
pepper to taste. Add to the yogurt
with the garlic and cochineal and stir
until well mixed. Pour into a large
bowl, add the fish, turn to coat
thoroughly and leave to marinate for
1 hour.

Pour boiling water into a roasting
pan to come halfway up the sides. Put
a grill rack in the pan and place the
marinated fish on the rack. Pour any
remaining marinade over the fish.

Cook in a preheated moderate
oven, 180°C (350°F), Gas Mark 4, for
15 minutes.

Garnish with coriander and lime
wedges and serve immediately.
Serves 2
NOTE: To serve 4 people, just add
2 more fish to the marinade.

STIR-FRIED FISH WITH VEGETABLES

500 g (1 lb) cod fillet,
  skinned
1 teaspoon salt
1 tablespoon oil
2 rashers back bacon,
  derinded and shredded
50 g (2 oz) frozen peas,
  cooked
50 g (2 oz) frozen
  sweetcorn, cooked
6 tablespoons chicken
  stock or water
2 teaspoons dry sherry
2 teaspoons soy sauce
1 teaspoon sugar
1 teaspoon cornflour,
  blended with 1 teaspoon
  water
spring onion fans to
  garnish (see right)

Cut the fish fillet into 2.5 cm (1 inch)
wide strips, sprinkle with the salt and
leave for 15 minutes.

Heat the oil in a frying pan, add the
fish and bacon and stir-fry for
3 minutes. Add the remaining
ingredients, except the blended
cornflour, and bring to the boil. Stir
in the blended cornflour and cook for
1 minute.

Garnish with spring onion fans and
serve immediately.

Serves 4

TO MAKE SPRING ONION FANS: Trim the
tops off the spring onions and remove
the root base. Shred carefully, leaving
2.5 cm (1 inch) attached. Immerse in
iced water until the spring onions
open out and curl.

MUSHROOM-STUFFED PLAICE

4 whole plaice, cleaned
1 tablespoon oil
1 onion, finely chopped
1 clove garlic, crushed
75 g (3 oz) fresh brown
    breadcrumbs
125 g (4 oz) mushrooms,
    finely chopped
1 tomato, skinned and
    chopped
1 teaspoon chopped
    marjoram
2 teaspoons chopped
    parsley
dash of Worcestershire
    sauce
watercress sprigs to
    garnish

Trim the fish by cutting the fins and tail with a sharp knife. With the white side uppermost, make an incision down the backbone of each fish. Working from each end of the cut in turn, on one half of the fish, cut about two thirds of the way around to form a pocket. Repeat on the other half.

Heat the oil in a pan, add the onion, garlic and breadcrumbs and fry until the breadcrumbs are crisp. Stir in the remaining ingredients and sauté for 2 minutes. Divide the filling between the prepared pockets.

Place the fish in a buttered oven-proof dish and cover with foil. Cook in a preheated moderately hot oven, 200°C (400°F), Gas Mark 6, for 20 to 30 minutes. Garnish with watercress and serve immediately with grilled tomatoes and mushrooms.
Serves 4 to 6

SWORDFISH PROVENÇALE

2 swordfish steaks
1 tablespoon sunflower oil
1 onion, sliced
750 g (1½ lb) tomatoes,
    thickly sliced
250 g (8 oz) green beans,
    cut in half
125 g (4 oz) green olives,
    stoned
2 tablespoons capers
2 teaspoons chopped
    oregano
MARINADE:
150 ml (¼ pint) dry
    white wine
4 tablespoons lemon juice
1 small onion, sliced
1 bay leaf
2 thyme sprigs
2 parsley sprigs
2 rosemary sprigs
2 cloves garlic, crushed
salt and pepper
TO GARNISH:
basil sprigs

Cut the swordfish steaks in half, place in a shallow dish and add the marinade ingredients, with salt and pepper to taste. Chill for several hours.

Remove the fish with a slotted spoon; reserve the marinade. Heat the oil in a large pan, add the fish and fry for 5 minutes. Transfer to a casserole dish.

Add the onion, tomatoes, beans, olives, capers, oregano and reserved marinade to the pan and cook, stirring, for 5 minutes. Transfer to the casserole and season with salt and pepper to taste.

Cook in a preheated moderate oven, 180°C (350°F), Gas Mark 4, for 35 to 40 minutes. Discard the bay leaf. Garnish with basil to serve.
Serves 4

HALIBUT WITH RHUBARB

250 g (8 oz) rhubarb, cut
   into 1 cm (½ inch)
   pieces
1 tablespoon soft brown
   sugar
1 tablespoon chopped mint
5 tablespoons dry white
   wine
2 halibut steaks
salt and pepper
mint sprigs to garnish

Place the rhubarb, sugar and mint in a casserole, then pour over the wine. Place the fish on top, and season with salt and pepper to taste.

Cover and cook in a preheated moderately hot oven, 200°C (400°F), Gas Mark 6, for 15 to 20 minutes, until tender.

Garnish with mint and serve immediately, with creamed potatoes.
Serves 2

SPINACH PANCAKES WITH CRAB

PANCAKE BATTER:
125 g (4 oz) wholewheat
   flour
½ teaspoon salt
1 egg, beaten
300 ml (½ pint) milk
125 g (4 oz) frozen
   chopped spinach,
   thawed
oil for shallow-frying
FILLING:
25 g (1 oz) butter
2 shallots, chopped
1 clove garlic, chopped
125 g (4 oz) mushrooms,
   sliced
25 g (1 oz) plain flour
300 ml (½ pint) milk
350 g (12 oz) crabmeat
4 tablespoons crème fraîche
4 tablespoons sherry
1 tablespoon grated
   Parmesan cheese
1 tablespoon chopped
   chervil
salt and pepper
TOPPING:
25 g (1 oz) butter, melted
1 tablespoon grated
   Parmesan cheese
TO GARNISH (optional):
whole prawns and dill

To make the batter, place the flour and salt in a bowl, add the egg and half the milk and beat until smooth. Beat in the remaining milk, then stir in the spinach.

Heat a little oil in a 15–18 cm (6–7 inch) frying pan. Pour in about 1½ tablespoons of the batter and cook until the mixture has set and the edges are golden brown. Turn the pancake over and cook the other side. Repeat with the remaining batter, stacking the cooked pancakes on a plate, interleaved with greaseproof paper.

To make the filling, melt the butter in a pan, stir in the shallots, garlic and mushrooms and sauté until soft. Stir in the flour and cook for 1 minute.

Remove from the heat and stir in the remaining ingredients, seasoning with salt and pepper to taste.

Divide the filling between the pancakes, placing it down the middle, and roll up. Place in a shallow oven-proof dish, brush with the melted butter and sprinkle with the cheese.

Cook in a preheated moderately hot oven, 200°C (400°F), Gas Mark 6, for 10 to 15 minutes, until crisp.

Garnish with whole prawns and dill leaves, if using, and serve at once.
Serves 4

PICKLED HERRINGS

6 herrings, cleaned,
  backbone removed, then
  cut in half lengthways
2 small onions, sliced and
  separated into rings
2 dill cucumbers, sliced
MARINADE:
300 ml (½ pint) cider
  vinegar
300 ml (½ pint) dry cider
1 teaspoon soft brown
  sugar
2 bay leaves
4 cloves
6 black peppercorns
6 allspice
2 blades of mace
½ teaspoon sea-salt
½ teaspoon cayenne
  pepper
TO GARNISH:
dill leaves

Place the marinade ingredients in a saucepan, bring to the boil then simmer for 10 minutes.

Lay the herring fillets, flesh side uppermost, on a board. Divide the onion rings and cucumber slices between each fillet, laying along the fish. Roll up from head to tail and secure with a wooden cocktail stick.

Arrange the herring rolls in an ovenproof dish and pour over the marinade. Sprinkle with any remaining onion rings.

Cover with a lid or foil and cook in a preheated moderate oven, 180°C (350°F), Gas Mark 4, for 30 minutes.

Leave in the marinade until cool, then place in the refrigerator. Chill for 1 to 2 days before serving.

Garnish with dill leaves and serve with crusty bread and a green salad.
Serves 6

PRAWNS IN GINGER SAUCE

8 spring onions, chopped
5 cm (2 inch) piece fresh
    root ginger, chopped
2 tablespoons dry sherry
2 tablespoons soy sauce
150 ml (¼ pint) chicken
    stock
salt and pepper
12 Mediterranean
    prawns, peeled

Place all the ingredients, except the prawns, in a saucepan, seasoning with salt and pepper to taste. Bring to the boil, then simmer for 2 minutes. Stir in the prawns, cover and cook for 3 minutes. Serve immediately, with rice or noodles.
Serves 4

SMOKED MACKEREL GOUGÈRE

25 g (1 oz) butter
1 onion, chopped
25 g (1 oz) plain flour
150 ml (¼ pint) milk
3 tablespoons dry cider
2 tablespoons natural
    yogurt
350 g (12 oz) smoked
    mackerel, flaked
3 tablespoons chopped
    watercress
1 small dessert apple,
    peeled and chopped
salt and pepper
CHOUX PASTRY:
300 ml (½ pint) water
50 g (2 oz) butter
175 g (6 oz) plain flour
4 eggs, beaten
75 g (3 oz) Cheddar
    cheese, grated
1 teaspoon dry mustard
TOPPING:
1 tablespoon fresh brown
    breadcrumbs
25 g (1 oz) flaked
    almonds, chopped
TO GARNISH:
apple slices tossed in
    lemon juice
mint leaves

Melt the butter in a pan, add the onion and fry until softened. Stir in the flour and milk, bring to the boil, stirring, then simmer for 3 minutes.

Remove from the heat and stir in the remaining ingredients, with salt and pepper to taste. Leave to cool.

To make the choux pastry, place the water and butter in a saucepan and heat gently until melted, then bring to the boil. Remove from the heat, add the flour and beat until smooth.

Return to the heat and beat for 40 seconds, until the mixture leaves the side of the pan and forms a ball.

Remove from the heat and allow to cool slightly, then beat in the eggs a little at a time, beating well after each addition to form a thick glossy dough. Stir in the cheese, mustard, and salt and pepper to taste.

Spoon the choux pastry around the edge of a shallow 1.75 litre (3 pint) ovenproof dish. Place the prepared filling in the centre and sprinkle with the breadcrumbs and almonds.

Cook in a preheated moderately hot oven, 200°C (400°F), Gas Mark 6, for 40 to 45 minutes, until risen and golden. Garnish with apple and mint and serve immediately.
Serves 4 to 6
NOTE: The filling can be made in advance if kept covered and chilled.

FAMILY MEALS

SUPPER HERRINGS

4 herrings, filleted
1 tablespoon made
   English mustard
salt and pepper
1 large onion, sliced
1 large cooking apple,
   peeled, cored and sliced
½ teaspoon chopped sage
750 g (1½ lb) potatoes,
   thinly sliced
150 ml (¼ pint) boiling
   water
sage leaves to garnish

Spread the cut side of the herrings with the mustard, and sprinkle with salt and pepper. Roll them up.

Place a layer of onion in a buttered gratin dish. Cover with a layer of apple and place the herrings on top. Sprinkle with the sage. Cover with the remaining onion and apple and top with a layer of potato.

Pour in the boiling water, cover with foil and cook in a preheated moderately hot oven, 200°C (400°F), Gas Mark 6, for 45 to 50 minutes.

Garnish with sage and serve immediately.
Serves 4

BAKED MACKEREL IN CIDER

1 kg (2 lb) cooking
  apples, peeled, cored
  and thinly sliced
5 tablespoons dry cider
150 g (5 oz) natural
  yogurt
5 tablespoons Dijon
  mustard
salt and pepper
4 mackerel, filleted
TO GARNISH:
lemon slices
parsley sprig

Spread the apples in a large buttered gratin dish.

Heat the cider gently and pour over the apples. Cover with foil and cook in a preheated moderately hot oven, 200°C (400°F), Gas Mark 6, for 15 minutes. Lower the temperature to 180°C (350°F), Gas Mark 4.

Meanwhile, mix the yogurt with the mustard, and salt and pepper to taste.

Arrange the mackerel in the dish and pour over the yogurt mixture. Return to the oven and cook for 30 minutes.

Garnish with lemon slices and parsley to serve.
Serves 4

QUICK-FRY SALMON

1 tablespoon sunflower oil
1 onion, chopped
500 g (1 lb) potatoes, par-
    boiled and diced
1 × 439 g (15½ oz) can
    salmon, drained and
    flaked
2 tablespoons chopped
    parsley
125 g (4 oz) frozen peas
pepper
parsley sprigs to garnish

Heat the oil in a pan, add the onion and sauté until soft and transparent.

Add the potatoes and fry for 5 minutes, stirring.

Stir in the salmon, parsley, peas, and pepper to taste. Fry gently for 5 minutes, until heated through. Garnish with parsley and serve immediately.

Serves 4

WHOLEWHEAT FISH CRUMBLE

750 g (1½ lb) halibut
300 ml (½ pint) milk
bouquet garni
salt and pepper
1 celery heart, cut into
    1 cm (½ inch) pieces
1 small fennel bulb, diced
2 leeks, sliced
1 carrot, sliced
1 teaspoon grated lemon
    rind
1 tablespoon lemon juice
150 ml (¼ pint) water
40 g (1½ oz) unsalted
    butter
40 g (1½ oz) plain flour
3 tablespoons crème fraîche
2 tablespoons chopped
    parsley
1 teaspoon chopped fennel
    leaves
TOPPING:
50 g (2 oz) unsalted
    butter
125 g (4 oz) wholewheat
    flour
75 g (3 oz) matured
    Cheddar cheese, grated
½ teaspoon cayenne
    pepper

Put the fish in a saucepan with the milk, bouquet garni, and salt and pepper to taste, cover and simmer for 10 to 15 minutes, until the fish flakes away from the skin. Remove with a slotted spoon, reserving the cooking liquid. Remove any skin and bones and flake the fish into large pieces.

Place the vegetables in a saucepan with the lemon rind, juice and water. Bring to the boil, then cover and simmer for 5 minutes, until just tender. Drain, reserving the cooking liquid, and set aside.

Melt the butter in a pan, stir in the flour and cook for 1 minute. Gradually stir in the reserved cooking liquids, bring to the boil and boil for 1 minute. Remove from the heat and stir in the crème fraîche, parsley, fennel leaves, fish and vegetables. Pour into a 1.2 litre (2 pint) pie dish.

Rub the butter into the flour until the mixture resembles breadcrumbs. Stir in the cheese and cayenne and sprinkle over the fish mixture.

Cook in a preheated moderately hot oven, 200°C (400°F), Gas Mark 6, for 20 minutes. Serve hot.

Serves 4 to 6

FISH FACES

150 ml (¼ pint) milk
150 ml (¼ pint) water
250 g (8 oz) haddock
   fillets
salt and pepper
500 g (1 lb) potatoes,
   boiled and mashed
1 × 213 g (7½ oz) can
   pink salmon, drained
   and flaked
125 g (4 oz) tomatoes,
   skinned and chopped
4 tablespoons chopped
   parsley
2 tablespoons natural
   yogurt
75 g (3 oz) fresh whole-
   wheat breadcrumbs
2 tablespoons grated cheese
25 g (1 oz) plain flour
1 egg, beaten
2 tablespoons oil
TO GARNISH:
olive slices
tomato strips
lemon slices

Bring the milk and water to the boil in a large pan, add the haddock and a little salt and pepper and simmer for 10 minutes, or until tender.

Remove any skin and bones from the haddock and flake the fish. Place in a bowl with the potato, salmon, tomato, half the parsley, yogurt, and salt and pepper to taste and mix well. Divide the mixture into 8 and shape each piece into an oval.

Mix together the breadcrumbs, cheese and remaining parsley. Dip the fish cakes into the flour, then the beaten egg, and finally into the breadcrumb mixture to coat completely.

Heat the oil in a frying pan, add the fish cakes and fry for 3 minutes on each side, until golden. Transfer to a warmed serving plate and garnish each fish cake with an olive slice for an eye, a tomato strip for a mouth and lemon slices, quartered, for its tail.

Makes 8

SARDINE PIZZA

1 × 150 g (6 oz) packet
  pizza base mix
1 × 120 g (4¼ oz) can
  sardines in oil, drained
  and mashed
1 × 397 g (14 oz) can
  tomatoes, drained and
  chopped
½ teaspoon chopped
  oregano
salt and pepper
1 green pepper, cored,
  seeded and sliced
50 g (2 oz) mushrooms,
  sliced
125 g (4 oz) Mozzarella
  cheese, sliced
1 × 50 g (1¾ oz) can
  anchovy fillets, drained
6 black olives

Make up the pizza mix according to packet directions. Roll into an 18 cm (7 inch) circle and place on a baking sheet.

Place the sardines, tomatoes, oregano, and salt and pepper to taste in a bowl and mix well to combine. Spoon onto the pizza base and arrange the green pepper and mushrooms attractively on top. Cover with the cheese slices.

Arrange the anchovies in a criss cross pattern on top and finish with the olives.

Cook in a preheated moderately hot oven, 200°C (400°F), Gas Mark 6, for 20 to 25 minutes.

Serve immediately, with a green salad.

Serves 4 to 6

VARIATION: Replace the sardines with 1 × 99 g (3½ oz) can tuna steak.

STUFFED PEPPERS

500 g (1 lb) cod fillets
300 ml (½ pint) boiling
  water
bouquet garni
½ onion
salt and pepper
1 tablespoon sunflower oil
1 onion, chopped
2 celery sticks, chopped
125 g (4 oz) brown rice
1 × 227 g (8 oz) can
  tomatoes
1 bay leaf
1 teaspoon chopped
  marjoram
150 ml (¼ pint) cold
  water
125 g (4 oz) peeled
  prawns
4 tablespoons frozen
  sweetcorn
4 green peppers
TO GARNISH:
marjoram sprigs
whole prawns in shell

Place the fish in a pan with the boiling water, bouquet garni, half-onion, and salt and pepper to taste. Cover and simmer for 10 to 15 minutes.

Remove with a slotted spoon, remove any skin and bones and flake the fish into chunks. Set aside.

Heat the oil in a frying pan, add the chopped onion and celery and fry for 2 minutes. Add the rice and fry for a further 3 minutes.

Stir in the tomatoes, with their juice, bay leaf, marjoram, and salt and pepper to taste. Pour in the cold water, bring to the boil, cover and simmer for 40 minutes, until rice is tender and liquid absorbed. Remove from the heat and stir in the flaked fish, prawns and sweetcorn.

Remove the top from each pepper and reserve. Remove the core and seeds, and trim the base to level. Blanch in a pan of boiling water for 2 minutes, drain and plunge into cold water. Drain well.

Divide the rice and fish mixture between the 4 peppers. Arrange in an ovenproof dish and replace the tops. Cook in a preheated moderate oven, 180°C (350°F), Gas Mark 4, for 15 minutes. Garnish with marjoram sprigs and prawns to serve.
Serves 4

FISH IN WHOLEWHEAT BREADCRUMBS

4 haddock fillets
2 tablespoons plain flour
125 g (4 oz) wholewheat
  breadcrumbs
2 tablespoons chopped
  parsley
salt and pepper
1 egg, beaten
oil for shallow-frying
TO GARNISH:
parsley sprigs
lemon wedges

Dip the fillets into the flour.

Mix together the breadcrumbs, parsley, and salt and pepper to taste on a plate.

Dip the fillets into the beaten egg, then into the breadcrumb mixture. Shallow-fry in hot oil until crisp and golden.

Garnish with parsley and lemon and serve with Tartare Sauce (see page 89).
Serves 4

CRISPY TOP COD

300 ml (½ pint) boiling
   water
bouquet garni
1 onion, roughly chopped
4 chunky cod fillets
75 g (3 oz) Cheddar
   cheese, grated
450 ml (¾ pint) White
   Sauce (see page 86)
2 × 25 g (1 oz) packets
   ready salted crisps
TO GARNISH:
parsley sprigs
lemon twists

Place the water, bouquet garni and
onion in a large pan, add the cod and
cook for 10 to 15 minutes, until
tender. Remove with a slotted spoon
and place in a shallow dish.

Stir the cheese into the hot sauce
until melted. Pour over the fish.
Roughly crush the crisps and sprinkle
over.

Cook under a preheated hot grill
for 2 to 3 minutes, until golden.
Garnish with parsley and lemon and
serve immediately.
Serves 4 to 6

39

MARINER'S PIE

450 ml (¾ pint) milk
1 bay leaf
2 lemon slices
salt and pepper
500 g (1 lb) whiting fillets
50 g (2 oz) butter
125 g (4 oz) button
   mushrooms, quartered
40 g (1½ oz) plain flour
3 tablespoons yogurt or
   soured cream
2 tablespoons chopped
   parsley
2 hard-boiled eggs,
   chopped
500 g (1 lb) potatoes,
   boiled and sliced
50 g (2 oz) Cheddar
   cheese, grated
TO GARNISH:
parsley sprigs

Put the milk, bay leaf, lemon slices, and salt and pepper to taste in a saucepan and bring to the boil. Add the fish and simmer for 10 to 15 minutes, until tender. Remove with a slotted spoon. Strain and reserve the liquid. Flake the fish, removing any skin or bones.

Melt the butter in a pan, add the mushrooms and cook for 2 minutes. Stir in the flour, cook for 1 minute, then gradually stir in the reserved liquid and bring to the boil.

Remove from the heat and stir in the fish, yogurt or soured cream, parsley and chopped egg. Check the seasoning and pour into a 1.2 litre (2 pint) pie dish. Arrange the potato on top, then sprinkle with the cheese.

Cook under a preheated moderate grill for 5 minutes, or in a preheated moderate oven, 180°C (350°F), Gas Mark 4, for 10 to 15 minutes.

Garnish with the parsley and serve immediately.
Serves 4

40

CREAMED COCONUT MONKFISH

125 g (4 oz) desiccated
  coconut
300 ml (½ pint) boiling
  water
750 g (1½ lb) monkfish
1 tablespoon oil
6 spring onions, chopped
3 green chillies, seeded
  and chopped
1 red pepper, cored, seeded
  and chopped
1 clove garlic, crushed
5 cm (2 inch) piece fresh
  root ginger, chopped
½ teaspoon ground cumin
½ teaspoon ground
  coriander
1 teaspoon grated lemon
  rind
1 tablespoon lime juice
1 tablespoon sherry
salt and pepper
TO GARNISH:
lime wedges
coriander leaves

Place the coconut in a bowl, pour over the boiling water and leave to infuse for 30 minutes. Strain and reserve the liquid, discarding the coconut.

Meanwhile, cut the fish into 5 cm (2 inch) cubes. Heat the oil in a large pan and stir in the remaining ingredients, except the fish, seasoning with salt and pepper to taste. Add the fish, pour on the coconut milk and bring to the boil, then simmer for 5 minutes.

Transfer to a warmed serving dish, garnish with lime and coriander, and serve with rice.
Serves 4

FISHERMAN'S PIE

350 ml (12 fl oz) milk
1 bay leaf
1 onion, quartered
350 g (12 oz) smoked
  haddock or cod
350 g (12 oz) fresh
  haddock or whiting
25 g (1 oz) unsalted
  butter
25 g (1 oz) plain flour
125 g (4 oz) peeled
  prawns
125 g (4 oz) frozen peas
2 tablespoons chopped
  parsley
salt and pepper
2 × 370 g (13 oz) packets
  wholewheat puff
  pastry, thawed
beaten egg to glaze
TO GARNISH:
orange wedges
watercress sprigs

Place the milk, bay leaf and onion in a large saucepan and bring to the boil. Add the fish and cook gently for 10 minutes, until tender. Remove with a slotted spoon. Make up the cooking liquid to 350 ml (12 fl oz) with water and set aside.

Remove the skin and bones from the fish and flake the flesh.

Melt the butter in a large pan, stir in the flour and cook for 1 minute. Gradually stir in the reserved cooking liquid until smooth, then bring to the boil. Remove from the heat and stir in the fish, prawns, peas, parsley, and salt and pepper to taste. Leave to cool.

Roll out half the pastry on a floured surface to an oval about 23 × 30 cm (9 × 12 inches). Place on a dampened baking sheet and pour on the cooled fish mixture. Roll out the remaining pastry to the same size and shape and place on top. Trim, reserving any left-over pastry for decoration. Dampen, seal and flute the edge. Make a small hole in the centre and decorate with pastry trimmings. Brush with beaten egg.

Bake in a preheated moderately hot oven, 200°C (400°F), Gas Mark 6, for 30 to 35 minutes. Lower the temperature to 180°C (350°F), Gas Mark 4, and bake for a further 20 minutes. Garnish with orange and watercress. Serve hot.
Serves 4 to 6

SKATE PARCELS

3 tablespoons sunflower
　oil
2 carrots, sliced into
　matchstick pieces
3 celery sticks, sliced
　lengthways
½ fennel bulb, sliced
　lengthways
8 spring onions, sliced
　lengthways
1 courgette, sliced
　lengthways
1 tablespoon soy sauce
1 tablespoon dry sherry
1 tablespoon tomato
　ketchup
salt and pepper
4 skate wings
orange twists to garnish

Heat 1 tablespoon of the oil in a
frying pan, add the vegetables and
stir-fry for 3 minutes.

　Add the soy sauce, sherry, tomato
ketchup, and salt and pepper to taste
and simmer for 2 minutes. Set aside.

　Heat the remaining oil in another
pan, add the skate wings and fry
quickly for 2 minutes on each side.

　Place each skate wing on a large
piece of foil and cover with the
vegetable mixture. Fold the foil over
to form a parcel and seal well.

　Place on a baking sheet and cook in
a preheated moderately hot oven,
200°C (400°F), Gas Mark 6, for 15 to
20 minutes, until tender.

　Garnish with orange twists and
serve immediately.
Serves 4

STARTERS AND SALADS

CARIBBEAN SCAMPI

350 g (12 oz) uncooked
   scampi
3 tablespoons plain flour
oil for deep-frying
50 g (2 oz) desiccated
   coconut
BATTER:
125 g (4 oz) plain flour
pinch of salt
2 teaspoons sunflower oil
7-8 tablespoons beer or
  tepid water
2 egg whites
TO GARNISH:
coriander sprig
lime wedges

First, make the batter. Sift the flour and salt into a bowl, then beat in the oil and beer or water to form a smooth thick batter.

Just before using, whisk the egg whites until soft peaks form, then gently fold into the batter mixture.

Toss the scampi in the flour, then dip into the batter to coat thickly and evenly.

Deep-fry a few at a time in the hot oil for 5 to 7 minutes, until crisp and golden. Drain on kitchen paper, then toss in the coconut.

Serve immediately, garnished with coriander and lime.
Serves 4

MOULES MARINIÈRE

2.25 litres (4 pints) fresh
   mussels
2 shallots, chopped
1 onion, chopped
50 g (2 oz) chopped
   parsley
300 ml (½ pint) dry
   white wine
50 g (2 oz) unsalted
   butter
salt and pepper
chopped parsley to garnish
   (optional)

Scrub and clean the mussels, removing any beards. Place in a large saucepan with the shallots, onion, parsley, wine and butter. Bring to the boil, cover and simmer for about 5 minutes, shaking the pan occasionally, until the shells open; discard any that do not. Remove the mussels with a slotted spoon, pile into a warmed serving bowl and keep hot.

Strain the cooking liquid into another pan. Bring to the boil and boil for 1 minute. Season with salt and pepper to taste, then pour over the mussels.

Garnish with parsley, if desired, and serve immediately, with crusty French bread.

Serves 4

MONKFISH KEBABS

500 g (1 lb) monkfish,
    cubed
2 green peppers, cored,
    seeded and cut into
    2.5 cm (1 inch) squares
1 × 227 g (8 oz) can
    pineapple pieces
1 tablespoon olive oil
250 g (8 oz) bean sprouts
1 tablespoon soy sauce
salt and pepper
2 spring onions, chopped
MARINADE:
150 ml (¼ pint) olive oil
1 small onion, chopped
2 cloves garlic, crushed
1 teaspoon Dijon mustard
2 teaspoons cider vinegar

Place the monkfish in a shallow dish. Mix together the marinade ingredients, pour over the fish and leave for 1 hour.

Blanch the green pepper in boiling water for 1 minute. Drain the pineapple and reserve the juice.

Thread the fish, green pepper and pineapple alternately on 8 kebab skewers. Cook under a preheated moderate grill for 5 to 6 minutes on each side, basting with the marinade.

Meanwhile, heat the oil in a large frying pan, add the bean sprouts and stir-fry for 1 to 2 minutes. Add the reserved pineapple juice, the soy sauce, and salt and pepper to taste and heat for 1 to 2 minutes. Transfer to a warmed serving dish and sprinkle with the spring onions.

Place the kebabs on the bean sprout mixture and serve immediately.
Serves 4

HUSS AND WATERCRESS SOUP

600 ml (1 pint) milk
bouquet garni
2 shallots, chopped
250 g (8 oz) huss,
    chopped
125 g (4 oz) watercress
142 ml (5 fl oz) single
    cream
TO GARNISH:
watercress sprigs
    (optional)
croûtons

Place the milk, bouquet garni and shallots in a saucepan, bring to the boil, then lower the heat. Add the huss and watercress and simmer for 8 to 10 minutes, until the fish flakes when tested with a knife. Place in an electric blender or food processor and work until smooth.

Return to the saucepan, stir in the cream and heat gently; do not allow to boil.

Serve in individual warmed soup bowls, garnished with watercress if using, and croûtons.
Serves 4

GRAVAD LAX

750 g-1 kg (1½-2 lb)
  salmon tailpiece, scaled
  and filleted

PICKLE:

1 heaped tablespoon sea
  salt
1 tablespoon sugar
1 teaspoon black
  peppercorns, crushed
1 tablespoon brandy
1 tablespoon chopped dill

TO GARNISH:

dill leaves
lime slices

Mix together the pickle ingredients in a small bowl and transfer a quarter of the mixture to a flat dish.

Place one salmon fillet, skin side down, in the pickle mixture. Spread half of the remaining pickle over the cut side of the salmon. Place the other piece of salmon, skin side up, on top.

Cover with the remaining pickle mixture, rubbing it into the skin. Cover with foil, lay a board on top and weight it down.

Chill for at least 12 hours before serving; it can be left for up to 5 days.

Drain well and slice the salmon either on the bias for smaller slices or parallel to the skin to obtain larger slices. Garnish with dill and lime slices and serve with Mustard Sauce (see page 88).

Serves 4 to 6

POTTED SHRIMPS

750 g (1½ lb) shrimps in
 shells, or 500 g (1 lb)
 shelled shrimps
250 g (8 oz) unsalted
 butter, clarified (see
 below)
¼ teaspoon cayenne
 pepper
½ teaspoon ground mace
½ teaspoon grated nutmeg
salt
TO GARNISH:
lemon slices
chervil sprigs

Shell the shrimps if necessary. Drain
the shrimps well and dry with kitchen
paper.

Put two thirds of the clarified
butter into a saucepan with the spices,
and salt to taste. Add the shrimps and
heat gently for a few minutes. Divide
between 4 to 6 cocotte or ramekin
dishes and pack down tightly. Chill
until set.

Heat the remaining clarified butter
until just melted, then pour evenly
over the shrimp mixture to make an
airtight seal. Cover and keep in the
refrigerator for at least a day to
develop the flavour.

Garnish each dish with a lemon
slice and chervil sprig. Serve with hot
wholewheat toast.

Serves 4 to 6

TO CLARIFY BUTTER: Melt the butter,
leave to settle, then strain through
muslin.

TARAMASALATA

175 g (6 oz) smoked cod's
  roe, chopped
113 g (4 oz) curd cheese
50 g (2 oz) fresh white
  breadcrumbs
2 tablespoons lemon juice
8-10 tablespoons olive oil
pepper
1 teaspoon lumpfish
  caviar to garnish

Place the cod's roe, cheese,
breadcrumbs and lemon juice in a
food processor or electric blender and
work until smooth.

Gradually add the olive oil with the
machine running, and blend until
smooth and creamy. Season with
pepper to taste. Chill for 2 hours.

Garnish with lumpfish caviar and
serve with toast.

Serves 4

SALMON AND MONKFISH MOUSSELINES

125 g (4 oz) asparagus
  spears, trimmed and
  blanched
50 g (2 oz) peeled prawns
MONKFISH FILLING:
300 g (10 oz) monkfish,
  off the bone and
  trimmed of membrane
2 tablespoons dry white
  wine
2 tablespoons crème
  fraîche
2 tablespoons chopped
  tarragon
1 tablespoon chopped
  chervil
salt and pepper
1 egg, beaten
SALMON FILLING:
300 g (10 oz) salmon
  fillet
2 tablespoons crème
  fraîche
dash of Tabasco

Grease 4 individual loaf tins 10 × 6 ×
4 cm (4 × 2½ × 1½ inches) with
butter. Arrange the asparagus and
prawns attractively in the tins.

Roughly chop the monkfish and
place in a food processor or electric
blender with the remaining monkfish
filling ingredients, adding salt and
pepper to taste and half the beaten
egg. Work until smooth and divide
between the 4 tins.

Place the salmon filling ingredients
and remaining beaten egg in the food
processor or electric blender and
work until smooth. Divide between
the 4 tins, placing on top of the
monkfish filling.

Cover each tin with foil and place
in a roasting pan. Pour in enough
boiling water to come half-way up
the tins. Cook in a preheated
moderate oven, 180°C (350°F), Gas
Mark 4, for 15 to 20 minutes or until
firm when touched.

Unmould the mousselines onto
individual serving plates and serve
warm with Hollandaise Sauce (see
page 90).

If preferred, chill for several hours,
then turn out 30 minutes before
required to come to room
temperature.

Serves 4

SCALLOPS WITH DILL AND LIME

juice of 2 limes
350 g (12 oz) queens (see below) or scallops
salt and pepper
2 tablespoons chopped dill
1 tablespoon chopped mint
1/4 cucumber, diced
2 teaspoons sunflower oil
TO GARNISH:
lime slices
mint sprigs

Pour the lime juice into a saucepan, add the queens or scallops, and salt and pepper to taste. Bring to the boil, then simmer for 2 to 3 minutes, until white in appearance.

Remove from the heat and allow to cool. Add the dill, mint, cucumber and oil and place in a serving dish. Chill for 2 hours to allow the flavours to develop.

Garnish with lime slices and mint sprigs and serve with hot wholewheat toast.

Serves 4

NOTE: Queens are smaller than scallops and are ideal for starter dishes.

MACKEREL AND SPINACH CANNELLONI

175 g (6 oz) smoked
  mackerel fillets, flaked
113 g (4 oz) cottage
  cheese
125 g (4 oz) frozen
  chopped spinach,
  thawed
salt and pepper
8 tubes cannelloni
300 ml (½ pint) Tomato
  Sauce (see page 89)
2 tablespoons grated
  Parmesan cheese

Mix together the fish, cheese, spinach, and salt and pepper to taste. Divide between the cannelloni and place in an ovenproof dish. Pour over the tomato sauce and sprinkle with the Parmesan cheese.

Cook in a preheated moderate oven, 180°C (350°F), Gas Mark 4, for 15 to 20 minutes. Serve hot with a green salad.
Serves 4

FRIED WHITEBAIT

3 tablespoons plain flour
½ teaspoon salt
¼ teaspoon paprika
500 g (1 lb) whitebait
oil for deep-frying
TO GARNISH:
chopped parsley
lemon wedges

Mix the flour with the salt and paprika and use to coat the whitebait.

Deep-fry the whitebait in batches in hot oil for 2 to 3 minutes, until lightly browned and crisp. Drain on kitchen paper and place on a warmed serving plate.

Sprinkle with parsley and garnish with lemon wedges. Serve immediately, with thin slices of brown bread and butter.
Serves 4

CREAMY HADDOCK AND LEEKS

250 g (8 oz) smoked
  haddock
65 g (2½ oz) butter
2 leeks, sliced
500 g (1 lb) potatoes,
  boiled and diced
142 ml (5 fl oz) soured
  cream
salt and pepper
1 tablespoon chopped
  parsley to garnish

Place the haddock on a plate over a saucepan of boiling water. Dot with 15 g (½ oz) of the butter, cover and steam for 10 minutes or until the fish flakes easily.

Melt the remaining butter in a large pan, add the leeks and cook for 5 minutes, until soft. Add the potatoes and fish, then stir in the soured cream, and salt and pepper to taste.

Garnish with the chopped parsley and serve hot.
Serves 4

HUSS SALAD

500 g (1 lb) huss fillets,
  skinned
300 ml (½ pint) dry
  white wine or water
1 onion, roughly chopped
1 bay leaf
salt and pepper
500 g (1 lb) new potatoes,
  boiled and halved
½ cucumber, diced
1 × 250 g (8 oz) jar
  pickled sweet baby
  beetroot, cubed
2 tablespoons capers
DRESSING:
150 ml (¼ pint) Fromage
  Frais
juice of ½ lemon
2 tablespoons chopped
  chives
1 tablespoon chopped
  chervil

Place the fish, wine or water, onion,
bay leaf, and salt and pepper to taste
in a pan and simmer for 10 to 15
minutes or until the fish flakes easily.
Drain, cool and cube the fish.

Place in a large bowl with the
potatoes, cucumber, beetroot and
capers.

Mix the dressing ingredients
together, with salt and pepper to
taste, pour over the salad and mix
well.
Serves 4

SCAMPI AND AVOCADO SALAD

1 tablespoon olive oil
salt and pepper
250 g (8 oz) scampi
1 avocado pear, peeled,
  stoned and thinly sliced
2 oranges, peeled and
  segmented
2 small heads of chicory,
  separated into leaves
DRESSING:
2 tablespoons olive oil
3 tablespoons orange juice
2 tablespoons lemon juice
1 tablespoon chopped
  chervil
1 teaspoon chopped chives

Heat the oil in a frying pan and
sprinkle in a little salt and pepper.
Add the scampi and sauté for 3 to 5
minutes, until white in appearance.
Remove with a slotted spoon; reserve
the oil for the dressing.

Arrange the avocado, orange and
chicory on individual serving plates,
with the scampi.

Put the dressing ingredients in a
screw-top jar. Add the reserved oil,
and salt and pepper to taste and shake
well. Pour over the salads and serve.

Alternatively, chop all the salad
ingredients, place in a serving bowl,
pour over the dressing and toss well.
Serves 4
NOTE: If you want to serve the salad as
a main course, increase the scampi to
500g (1 lb).

KIWI TROUT SALAD

175 g (6 oz) smoked trout
2 dessert apples, cored
1 kiwi fruit, sliced
50 g (2 oz) flaked
  almonds, toasted
2 tablespoons soured
  cream
1 teaspoon lemon juice
2 tablespoons chopped
  mint
pepper
4 mint sprigs to garnish

Remove the skin and bones from the trout. Flake the fish into bite-sized pieces and place in a bowl.

Chop the apples and add to the fish with the kiwi fruit, almonds, soured cream, lemon juice, chopped mint, and pepper to taste.

Mix well, divide between 4 serving plates and garnish with a mint sprig.
Serves 4
NOTE: If you want to serve this as a main course, double the ingredients.

AVOCADO-STUFFED RAINBOW TROUT

4 rainbow trout, cleaned
   and gutted
sunflower oil for brushing
STUFFING:
1 ripe avocado pear,
   peeled, stoned and
   chopped
1 teaspoon lemon juice
25 g (1 oz) pistachio nuts,
   finely chopped
1 tablespoon clear honey
1 tablespoon soy sauce
salt and pepper
TO GARNISH:
lime slices
coriander leaves

Mix all the stuffing ingredients together, adding salt and pepper to taste. Divide the stuffing between the trout, placing it in the cavity of each fish.

Place the trout in a roasting pan, brush with sunflower oil and cover with foil. Cook in a preheated moderate oven, 180°C (350°F), Gas Mark 4, for 20 minutes or until tender.

Transfer to a warmed serving dish. Garnish with lime and coriander and serve immediately.
Serves 4

STUFFED MUSSELS

4 dozen fresh mussels,
   scrubbed clean
salt
2 lemon slices
2 teaspoons lemon juice
125 g (4 oz) butter,
   softened
3 cloves garlic, crushed
1 shallot, finely chopped
2 tablespoons chopped
   parsley
3 tablespoons fresh
   wholewheat
   breadcrumbs
TO GARNISH:
parsley sprigs
lemon wedges

Place the mussels in a pan of boiling salted water, add the lemon slices, cover and cook for about 7 minutes, until the mussels have opened. Remove with a slotted spoon, discarding any that have not opened. Remove the empty top shell from the mussel.

Beat the remaining ingredients together and spread the mixture on top of the mussels.

Place on a baking sheet and cook in a preheated moderately hot oven, 200°C (400°F), Gas Mark 6, for 5 minutes, until golden.

Arrange on a warmed serving dish, garnish with parsley and lemon and serve with crusty French bread.
Serves 4

PRAWN TARTLETS

1 × 215 g (7½ oz)
  packet frozen
  wholewheat shortcrust
  pastry, thawed
3 tablespoons mayonnaise
3 tablespoons soured cream
1 tablespoon tomato
  ketchup
½ teaspoon Tabasco
1 teaspoon cayenne pepper
2 tablespoons chopped
  chives
salt and pepper
175 g (6 oz) peeled
  prawns
7.5 cm (3 inch) piece
  cucumber, diced
2 tomatoes, skinned and
  chopped
2 hard-boiled eggs,
  chopped
dill leaves to garnish

Roll out the pastry on a floured surface to a 5 mm (¼ inch) thickness. Using a 7.5 cm (3 inch) fluted cutter, cut out 24 circles and use to line 2 patty trays. Prick the pastry well and 'bake blind' in a preheated moderate oven, 180°C (350°F), Gas Mark 4, for 10 to 15 minutes, until firm. Cool on a wire rack.

Mix together the mayonnaise, soured cream, tomato ketchup, Tabasco, cayenne, chives, and salt and pepper to taste. Add the remaining ingredients and stir well to mix. Check the seasoning.

Spoon the mixture into the cooked pastry cases. Arrange on a warmed serving dish and garnish with herbs to serve.
Makes 24

SCALLOP AND PRAWN BROCHETTES

150 ml (¼ pint) dry
  white wine
1 tablespoon raspberry
  vinegar
1 tablespoon chopped dill
  weed
½ teaspoon salt
12 large scallops
1½-2 cucumbers, peeled
  and cut into 1 cm
  (½ inch) slices
8 Mediterranean prawns
15 g (½ oz) butter,
  melted
TO GARNISH:
tomato quarters
basil leaves

Place the wine, vinegar, dill weed and salt in a large pan, bring to simmering point and add the scallops and cucumber. Simmer for 1 to 2 minutes, then remove with a slotted spoon; reserve the cooking liquid.

Place a prawn at one end of 4 long kebab skewers, arrange the scallops and cucumber alternately on the skewers, then add another prawn.

Brush with the butter and cook under a preheated high grill, or on a barbecue, for about 3 minutes on each side, basting frequently with the reserved cooking liquid.

Arrange the brochettes on a warmed serving dish. Garnish with tomato and basil and serve with Piquant Tomato Sauce (see page 91).
Serves 4

ICED CUCUMBER AND PRAWN SOUP

25 g (1 oz) butter
1 cucumber, chopped
2 shallots, chopped
300 ml (½ pint) milk
2 cloves garlic, crushed
1 bay leaf
salt and pepper
1 tablespoon chopped mint
1 tablespoon chopped
    chives
250 g (8 oz) peeled
    prawns
284 ml (10 fl oz) single
    cream
TO GARNISH:
mint sprigs
cucumber slices
peeled prawns

Melt the butter in a saucepan, add the cucumber and shallots, cover and cook gently for 5 minutes, until softened but not brown.

Add the milk, garlic, bay leaf, and salt and pepper to taste, and simmer for 10 minutes. Remove the bay leaf. Pour the soup into an electric blender or food processor and work until smooth. Pour into a soup tureen and stir in the herbs, prawns and cream. Chill for 2 hours.

Garnish with mint, cucumber slices and prawns to serve.

Serves 4

VARIATION: This soup could also be served warm: stir in the herbs, prawns and cream as above then heat gently; do not boil.

MONKFISH AND MELON SALAD

1 kg (2 lb) monkfish, cut
  into strips
8 scallops, cut in half,
  coral separated
1 onion, chopped
2 lemon or lime slices
bouquet garni
150 ml (¼ pint) dry cider
150 ml (¼ pint) water
salt and pepper
SALAD:
1 tablespoon sunflower oil
2 shallots, chopped
6 spring onions, chopped
2.5 cm (1 inch) piece fresh
  root ginger, chopped
½ teaspoon ground ginger
½ teaspoon paprika
4 celery sticks, chopped
4 tablespoons soured cream
4 tablespoons mayonnaise
2 tablespoons chopped
  mint
1 honeydew melon
TO GARNISH:
½ teaspoon paprika
lettuce leaves

Place the fish, including the scallop
coral, in a pan. Add the remaining
ingredients, with salt and pepper to
taste, bring to the boil, then simmer
for 5 minutes. Drain immediately and
leave to cool.

Heat the oil in a pan, add the
shallots, spring onions and chopped
ginger and sauté for 2 minutes.

Stir in the ground ginger, paprika
and celery and cook for 1 minute.
Place in a bowl and leave to cool.

Stir in the soured cream,
mayonnaise, mint, fish, and salt and
pepper to taste.

Halve the melon and discard the
seeds. Scoop the flesh into balls,
using a melon baller, or cut into
cubes, and add to the fish mixture.

Transfer to a serving bowl and chill
for 30 minutes, or until required.
Sprinkle with paprika and garnish
with lettuce to serve.

Serves 4 to 6

NOTE: If preferred, return the salad to
the emptied melon shells to serve.

SMOKED EEL MOUSSE

350 g (12 oz) smoked eel
125 g (4 oz) cottage
    cheese
142 ml (5 fl oz) soured
    cream
2 teaspoons grated lemon
    rind
1 tablespoon lemon juice
2 tablespoons chopped
    parsley
salt and pepper
TO GARNISH:
curly endive leaves
cucumber slices
radish slices

Remove the skin and bones from the eel and flake the fish.

Place in an electric blender or food processor, add the remaining ingredients, with salt and pepper to taste, and work until smooth. Transfer to a bowl and chill until required.

Spoon the mousse onto individual serving plates. Garnish with endive, cucumber and radishes to serve.
Serves 4

POACHED SALMON TROUT

This is an alternative method of cooking a salmon trout if you do not have a fish kettle.

1 salmon trout, weighing
    about 1 kg (2 lb),
    cleaned and gutted
1 bay leaf
1 lemon, sliced
1 teaspoon salt
12 black peppercorns
300 ml (½ pint) dry
    white wine
TO GARNISH:
½ × 25 g (1 oz) packet
    aspic powder
2 lemons, sliced
2 limes, sliced
small bunch of dill
½ packet of watercress

Line a large roasting pan with foil and brush with oil. Place the salmon trout on the foil, curving the fish slightly. Place the bay leaf and lemon slices on the fish, then sprinkle with the salt and peppercorns. Pour over the wine. Bring the edges of foil together and seal to make a loose parcel.

Cook in a preheated cool oven, 150°C (300°F), Gas Mark 2, for 30 minutes. Leave to cool in the pan.

Unwrap the fish, carefully remove the skin, leaving some around the head and tail, and place on a serving dish.

Make up the aspic to 300 ml (½ pint) according to packet directions. Coat the fish with a thin layer of aspic jelly. Cut most of the lemon and lime slices into quarters and arrange down the centre of the fish with the dill. Brush the lemon and lime slices with a little aspic jelly.

Chill in the refrigerator until set. Garnish with any remaining lemon and lime slices and watercress.
Serves 4

RED MULLET IN VINE LEAVES

6 vine leaves
2 red mullet, weighing
    about 250 g (8 oz)
    each, scaled and washed
sunflower oil for brushing
STUFFING:
1 large tomato, chopped
2 anchovy fillets, chopped
2 tablespoons chopped
    parsley
1 tablespoon chopped basil
1 clove garlic, crushed
salt and pepper
TO GARNISH:
4 anchovies
2 black olives

Mix the stuffing ingredients together, seasoning with salt and pepper, and divide between 2 vine leaves, spreading over one side of each leaf.

Arrange the vine leaves overlapping in two groups of three, with a covered vine leaf forming the centre of each group. Place the mullet on top and wrap the vine leaves around.

Place in a roasting pan, brush with oil and cook in a preheated moderately hot oven, 200°C (400°F), Gas Mark 6, for 15 minutes.

Transfer to a warmed serving dish and top with the anchovies and olives.
Serves 2

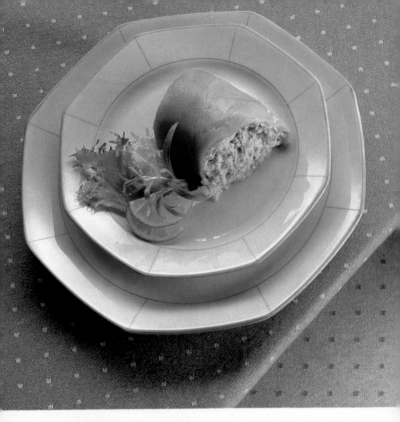

SALMON MOUSSE

250 g (8 oz) smoked
    salmon slices
1 × 439 g (15½ oz) can
    red salmon
142 ml (5 fl oz) single
    cream
8 tablespoons crème
    fraîche
½ cucumber, finely diced
2 tablespoons chopped
    tarragon
2 eggs, separated
¼ teaspoon cayenne
    pepper
salt and pepper
15 g (½ oz) gelatine,
    soaked in 3 tablespoons
    cold water
watercress or curly endive
lime slices and tarragon
    leaves to garnish

Line a 1.25 litre (2 ¼ pint) ring mould
with the smoked salmon.

Drain and flake the red salmon,
then mix with the cream, crème
fraîche, cucumber, tarragon, egg
yolks, cayenne, and salt and pepper to
taste.

Heat the gelatine gently until
dissolved, then carefully stir a little at
a time into the salmon mixture.

Whisk the egg whites until soft
peaks form, then gently fold into the
salmon mixture. Pour into the ring
mould and chill for several hours,
until set.

To serve, invert the ring mould
onto a serving plate and fill the centre
with watercress or curly endive.
Garnish with lime and tarragon.
Serves 6 to 8

GRAPEFRUIT AND PRAWN SALAD

1 tablespoon sunflower oil
1 large onion, finely
    chopped
250 g (8 oz) peeled
    prawns
2 tablespoons lemon juice
4 tablespoons dry white
    wine
salt and pepper
4 tablespoons mayonnaise
1 teaspoon Tabasco
½ teaspoon cayenne
    pepper
2 ruby red grapefruit,
    peeled and segmented
1 red pepper, cored, seeded
    and diced
1 lettuce

Heat the oil in a pan, add the onion
and sauté until transparent. Add the
prawns, lemon juice, wine, and salt
and pepper to taste and simmer for
5 minutes.

Leave to cool slightly, then remove
the prawns and onion with a slotted
spoon and place in a bowl. Add the
mayonnaise, Tabasco and cayenne
and stir lightly to mix.

Cut each grapefruit segment in half
and add to the prawn mixture with
the yellow pepper.

To serve, divide between 4 serving
plates, lined with lettuce leaves.
Serves 4

CURRIED PRAWN RING

350 g (12 oz) long grain
  rice
salt
few saffron threads
1 tablespoon sunflower oil
1 tablespoon curry powder
8 spring onions, chopped
1 red pepper, cored, seeded
  and chopped
50 g (2 oz) pine nuts
75 g (3 oz) sultanas
250 g (8 oz) peeled
  prawns
DRESSING:
4 tablespoons olive oil
2 tablespoons white wine
  vinegar
1 teaspoon dry mustard
1 teaspoon sugar
2 tablespoons chopped
  coriander
TO GARNISH:
orange wedges
celery leaves

Cook the rice in boiling salted water, with the saffron added, for about 20 minutes, until the rice is tender and the liquid absorbed.

Meanwhile, place the dressing ingredients in a screw-top jar and shake well to blend.

Drain the rice, place in a bowl and stir in the dressing while still warm. Set aside to cool slightly.

Heat the oil in a pan, add the curry powder, spring onions, red pepper, pine nuts and sultanas and cook, stirring, for 1½ minutes. Add to the rice and leave until completely cold.

Stir in the prawns, then spoon the mixture into a lightly oiled 1.5 litre (2½ pint) ring mould, pressing down well. Chill until required.

To serve, invert the ring onto a serving plate and garnish with orange wedges and celery leaves.
Serves 4 to 6

JOHN DORY FILLETS

25 g (1 oz) plain flour
salt and pepper
6 John Dory fillets
175 g (6 oz) butter
350 g (12 oz)
  mushrooms, sliced
1 clove garlic, crushed
8 tablespoons double
  cream
1 teaspoon lemon juice
TO GARNISH:
parsley sprigs
lemon wedges

Season the flour with salt and pepper and use to coat the fish.

Heat 125 g (4 oz) of the butter in a small pan until bubbling. Line a sieve with muslin and pour the butter through this into a frying pan. Add the fish and fry gently for 3 minutes on each side. Keep warm.

Melt the remaining butter in another pan, add the mushrooms and garlic, cover and simmer for 8 minutes. Stir in the cream, lemon juice, and salt and pepper to taste and heat gently.

Arrange the fish on a warmed serving dish and pour over the sauce. Garnish with parsley and lemon wedges to serve.
Serves 6

SEA BASS BAKED IN SPINACH

1 sea bass, weighing about
    750 g (1½ lb), cleaned
    and gutted
250 g (8 oz) spinach
15 g (½ oz) butter,
    melted
2 shallots, chopped
150 ml (¼ pint) dry
    white wine
STUFFING:
50 g (2 oz) fresh
    breadcrumbs
15 g (½ oz) butter,
    melted
2 tablespoons chopped
    chervil
1 tablespoon each chopped
    tarragon and basil
1 tablespoon lemon juice
salt and pepper
TO GARNISH:
3 orange slices, quartered

Mix the stuffing ingredients together,
seasoning with salt and pepper to
taste, and use to stuff the fish cavity.

Put the spinach in a colander in a
bowl and pour over boiling water.
Drain thoroughly.

Wrap the stuffed bass in the
blanched spinach, leaving the head
and tail exposed.

Pour the melted butter over the
base of a gratin dish, sprinkle in the
shallots and place the fish on top.
Pour over the wine.

Cover with foil and cook in a
preheated moderately hot oven,
200°C (400°F), Gas Mark 6, for
30 minutes.

Transfer to a warmed serving dish,
garnish with quartered orange slices
and serve with a sauce (see pages 84–
91) if preferred.

Serves 2

FISH CASSEROLE

1 dozen mussels, cleaned
salt and pepper
1 monkfish, cleaned and
   filleted
2 squid, cleaned and ink
   sac removed
2 tablespoons oil
2 onions, chopped
2 carrots, thinly sliced
6 celery sticks, sliced
2 cloves garlic, crushed
1 × 397 g (14 oz) can
   tomatoes
2 teaspoons sugar
2 tablespoons lemon juice
2 tablespoons lime juice
2 tablespoons chopped
   coriander
bouquet garni
150 ml (¼ pint) dry cider
few drops of Tabasco
4 scallops, cleaned and cut
   in half horizontally
3 small red mullet, scaled
   and cleaned
chopped coriander to
   garnish

Place the mussels in a pan of boiling salted water and cook for about 7 minutes, until they open; discard any that do not open.

Cut the monkfish into 2.5 cm (1 inch) chunks. Cut the squid into thin slices; leave the tentacles in small pieces.

Heat the oil in a large pan, add the onions, carrots, celery and garlic and sauté for 4 minutes. Add the remaining ingredients, except the fish, with salt and pepper to taste, and bring to the boil. Add all the fish except the mussels, cover and simmer for 15 to 20 minutes, until the fish is cooked. Discard the bouquet garni.

Stir in the mussels and transfer to a warmed serving dish. Sprinkle with coriander and serve immediately.
Serves 6

SOLE VÉRONIQUE

8 Dover sole fillets
2 shallots, finely sliced
2 button mushrooms, finely sliced
1 bay leaf
1 parsley sprig
4 lemon slices
150 ml (¼ pint) dry white wine
4 tablespoons water
150 ml (¼ pint) milk (approximately)
25 g (1 oz) butter
25 g (1 oz) plain flour
142 ml (5 fl oz) double cream
1 teaspoon lemon juice
salt and pepper
175 g (6 oz) green grapes, peeled, cut in half and pips removed

Place the fish in a buttered ovenproof dish and sprinkle with the shallots and mushrooms. Add the bay leaf, parsley and lemon slices, and pour in the wine and water.

Cover with foil and cook in a preheated moderate oven, 180°C (350°F), Gas Mark 4, for 15 to 20 minutes, until tender.

Transfer the fish to a heatproof serving dish; keep warm.

Strain the cooking liquid into a small pan, bring to the boil and boil rapidly until reduced by half. Pour into a measuring jug and make up to 300 ml (½ pint) with the milk.

Melt the butter in a pan, stir in the flour and cook for 1 minute. Gradually stir in the reserved cooking liquid and milk mixture, bring to the boil, then simmer for 2 to 3 minutes. Stir in the cream, lemon juice, and salt and pepper to taste and bring to just below boiling point.

Remove from the heat and stir in two thirds of the grapes. Pour over the fish. Place under a preheated moderate grill for 1 minute to brown.

Garnish with the remaining grapes.
Serves 4

BRILL WITH PEAR

1 × 213 g (7½ oz) can pear halves in natural juice
4 brill or small turbot fillets
1 egg yolk
2 tablespoons chopped tarragon
1 tablespoon chopped parsley
1 teaspoon grated lemon rind
salt and pepper
142 ml (5 fl oz) single cream

Drain the pears and cut each piece in half. Wrap one fish fillet around each pear quarter. Place in a buttered ovenproof dish, just large enough to hold the fillets.

Beat the egg yolk, herbs, lemon rind, and salt and pepper to taste into the cream. Pour over the fish.

Cover with foil and cook in a preheated moderate oven, 180°C (350°F), Gas Mark 4, for 25 minutes or until tender. Serve hot.
Serves 4

BARBECUED SARDINES

These are excellent to serve at barbecue parties. They can, of course, also be cooked under a traditional grill.

16 fresh sardines, cleaned
MARINADE:
8 tablespoons lemon juice
2 tablespoons lime juice
3 cloves garlic, crushed
1 teaspoon paprika
1 teaspoon ground ginger
1 teaspoon ground cumin
1 teaspoon tomato purée
TO GARNISH:
lime slices
basil sprigs

Place the sardines in a flat dish. Mix the marinade ingredients together and pour over the fish. Leave to marinate in the refrigerator for 1 hour. Remove with a slotted spoon, reserving the marinade.

Line a grill pan with greased foil and place the sardines in the pan.

Cook under a preheated grill for 5 minutes on each side, basting with the marinade. Garnish with lime and basil. Accompany with Spicy Gooseberry Sauce (see page 88).
Serves 8

GOUJONS OF SOLE

2 Dover sole, skinned and
    filleted
50 g (2 oz) hazelnuts,
    finely chopped
125 g (4 oz) fresh
    wholewheat
    breadcrumbs
25 g (1 oz) plain flour
salt and pepper
1-2 eggs, beaten
oil for deep-frying
TO GARNISH:
parsley sprigs
orange segments

Cut the sole diagonally into strips
about 2.5 cm (1 inch) wide.

Mix together the hazelnuts and
breadcrumbs in a bowl.

Season the flour with salt and
pepper and use to coat the fish. Dip
into the beaten egg, then roll in the
breadcrumb mixture to coat
completely. Chill for about
30 minutes.

Deep-fry in hot oil, a few at a time,
for 2 minutes, until crisp and golden.
Drain on kitchen paper and place in a
warmed serving dish.

Garnish with parsley and orange
and serve immediately, accompanied
by Tartare Sauce (see page 89) and a
crisp green salad.
Serves 2 to 4

SOLE FILLETS WITH COURGETTES

50 g (2 oz) unsalted
  butter
350 g (12 oz) small
  courgettes, thinly sliced
salt and pepper
1 large tomato, skinned,
  seeded and chopped
4 Dover sole fillets
2 tablespoons lemon juice
1 tablespoon chopped basil
1 tablespoon fresh
  breadcrumbs
basil leaves to garnish

Melt half the butter in a pan, add the courgettes, and salt and pepper to taste and sauté for 3 minutes.

Add the tomato and continue cooking for 3 minutes, stirring occasionally.

Place the sole fillets in a gratin dish, dot with the remaining butter, and season with salt and pepper to taste. Pour over the lemon juice and sprinkle with the basil.

Pour the tomato and courgette mixture evenly over the fish and sprinkle with the breadcrumbs. Cook in a preheated moderately hot oven, 200°C (400°F), Gas Mark 6, for 10 to 15 minutes, until the fish is tender and the breadcrumbs crisp and golden.

Garnish with basil to serve.
Serves 2 or 4

OYSTERS

Oysters are very good on their own – *au naturel*. To ensure they are at their freshest, open them when you are about to serve the dish.

To open oysters, use a special oyster knife, if possible, or a round short-bladed knife; don't use a good sharp knife – you'll ruin it.

To protect your palm from the rough-edged shells, scrub them first and place a cloth in your palm. Holding the oyster over a bowl to catch the juice, insert the knife into the hinge and twist around between the shells to prise open. When breaking the shell open, try to keep the oyster in one piece by cutting the two muscles which lie above and below it.

To serve oysters *au naturel*, serve them on the flat shell on a bed of crushed ice, garnished with seaweed if possible for authenticity. Season lightly with salt and pepper and serve with lemon wedges and brown bread and butter.

OYSTERS À LA CRÈME

12 oysters
15 g (½ oz) butter
1 shallot, finely chopped
1 teaspoon chopped
    chervil
142 ml (5 fl oz) double
    cream
salt and pepper
25 g (1 oz) Gruyère
    cheese, grated
1 tablespoon dried
    breadcrumbs
chervil sprigs and lemon
    wedges to garnish

Open the oysters as described opposite. Return the oysters to the deeper rounded shell and arrange on a baking sheet, keeping them level with foil.

Melt the butter in a small pan, add the shallot and sauté until soft. Stir in the chervil, cream, and salt and pepper to taste and gently bring to the boil. Remove from the heat and stir in the cheese.

Cover each oyster with the sauce and sprinkle with the breadcrumbs.

Place under a preheated moderate grill for 2 minutes, until golden brown. Garnish with chervil and lemon and serve immediately.
Serves 2 to 4

OYSTERS WITH SMOKED SALMON

12 oysters
75 g (3 oz) smoked
    salmon, finely chopped
½ × 397 g (14 oz) can
    artichoke hearts,
    drained and finely
    chopped
25 g (1 oz) Gruyère
    cheese, grated
2 tablespoons dried
    breadcrumbs
pepper
HERB BUTTER:
75 g (3 oz) butter,
    softened
1 tablespoon chopped
    chervil
1 tablespoon chopped
    tarragon
2 teaspoons lemon juice
TO GARNISH:
lime wedges
tarragon leaves

First make the herb butter by beating all the ingredients together in a small bowl.

Open the oysters as described opposite. Return the oysters to the deeper rounded shell.

Place a little chopped salmon and artichoke on each oyster and dot with the herb butter. Sprinkle with the cheese, breadcrumbs, and pepper to taste.

Place on a baking sheet, balancing the oyster shells with foil if necessary, and cook in a preheated moderately hot oven, 200°C (400°F), Gas Mark 6, for 15 minutes. Alternatively, place under a preheated moderate grill for 10 to 15 minutes, until golden.

Transfer to a warmed serving dish, garnish with lime wedges and tarragon leaves and serve with brown bread and butter.
Serves 2 to 4

DRESSED CRAB

These days, dressed crab is quite readily available in the shops. However if you should have to cook and dress a live crab, here's how to go about it.

To Cook a Crab
Weigh the crab, if possible!

Have ready a large saucepan full of boiling salted water: use 175 g (6 oz) salt to 2-2.5 litres (3½-4 pints) water. Add a bay leaf, 5 peppercorns, 1 sliced onion, and 2 sliced celery sticks.

Put the crab in the water, cover the pan and bring to simmering point. Cook, allowing 15 minutes for the first 500 g (1 lb) and 8 minutes for each additional 500 g (1 lb). Remove from the pan and leave until cool.

To Dress a Crab
1. Place the crab on its back. Using a twisting action, remove the legs and claws from the body and set aside.
2. To separate the body, have the tail flap towards you. Hold the shell firmly with your fingers and, using your thumbs, push the body upwards until it becomes loosened, then separate from the shell.
3. Remove and discard the intestines or stomach bag and the grey feathery gills known as 'dead man's fingers'.
4. Spoon out the brown meat from the shell and place in a dish.
5. Cut the body in half. Using a thin skewer, dig out the white meat from the crevices. This may take time and patience, but is well worth it. Place in a separate dish.
6. Carefully crack open the reserved claws and legs using the back of a wooden spoon or a rolling pin and remove all the white meat; don't hit too hard or you will break up the meat. Add to the other white meat.
7. Trim the crab shell by tapping gently with a spoon around the natural marked line on the shell. Clean the shell ready for serving.

To Serve a Crab
Finely chop the white meat and season to taste with salt and pepper, cayenne pepper and 1 teaspoon dry white wine or cider vinegar.

Mix the brown meat with salt and pepper to taste, 1 teaspoon gin (optional), and 1 tablespoon finely chopped parsley (optional).

Place the brown meat in the centre of the shell and the white meat on either side. Garnish with chopped hard-boiled egg yolk and white, and 2 tablespoons finely chopped parsley, as shown.

Serve with an avocado and lettuce salad and mayonnaise.
Serves 2 to 4, depending on size of crab.

DEVILLED CRAB

2 crabs
142 ml (5 fl oz) double
    cream or crème fraîche
1 teaspoon Dijon mustard
2 teaspoons anchovy
    essence
1 teaspoon Worcestershire
    sauce
1/2 teaspoon cayenne
    pepper
1 teaspoon lemon juice
2 tablespoons chopped
    parsley
1 teaspoon chopped
    marjoram
125 g (4 oz) tomatoes,
    skinned and chopped
2 tablespoons dry sherry
salt and pepper
2 tablespoons fresh
    breadcrumbs, toasted
2 tablespoons finely grated
    Cheshire cheese
TO GARNISH:
watercress
cucumber slices

Cook and dress the crabs as described on page 76 and place all the meat in a large bowl. Stir in the cream or crème fraîche, mustard, anchovy essence, Worcestershire sauce, cayenne, lemon juice, parsley, marjoram, tomatoes, sherry, and salt and pepper to taste.

Brush the cleaned crab shells, inside and out, with oil. Divide the mixture between the shells; put any leftover mixture in a ramekin dish. Sprinkle with the breadcrumbs and cheese and cook in a preheated moderately hot oven, 200°C (400°F), Gas Mark 6, for 15 to 20 minutes, until golden brown.

To serve, place on a bed of lettuce and garnish with watercress and cucumber slices.

Serves 4

CRAB AND HERB MOUSSE

250 g (8 oz) crabmeat,
  fresh, frozen or canned
2 tablespoons finely grated
  Cheddar cheese
142 ml (5 fl oz) double
  cream
2 tablespoons chopped
  tarragon
1 tablespoon chopped
  chervil
1 tablespoon chopped basil
1 tablespoon lemon juice
1 tablespoon tomato
  ketchup
salt and pepper
15 g (½ oz) gelatine,
  soaked in 3 tablespoons
  cold water
2 egg whites
TO GARNISH:
cucumber slices
whole prawn in shell

Flake the crabmeat finely and place in a bowl. Stir in the cheese, cream, herbs, lemon juice, tomato ketchup, and salt and pepper to taste.

Heat the gelatine gently until dissolved, then carefully fold into the crab mixture.

Whisk the egg whites until soft peaks form, then fold into the crab mixture using a metal spoon.

Spoon the mixture into an 18–20 cm (7-8 inch) round cake tin or mould and chill for several hours, until set.

To serve, invert the mould onto a serving plate and garnish with cucumber slices and a whole prawn.
Serves 6

LOBSTERS

Lobsters are usually sold ready-cooked, but ideally they should be purchased alive. The shells are then greyish-blue – they turn their characteristic bright red colour in cooking. Smaller lobsters – about 750 g-1 kg (1½-2 lb) – have the best flavour. When selecting for buying, choose a lobster which feels heavy for its size.

To Cook a Lobster

Have ready a large saucepan full of boiling salted water: use 175 g (6 oz) salt to about 2 litres (3½ pints) water. Put the lobster in the water, cover the pan and bring to simmering point. Alternatively, if serving the lobster plain, cook in a court-bouillon (see page 11). Cook, allowing 12-15 minutes for the first 500 g (1 lb) and 10 minutes for each additional 500 g (1 lb).

To Prepare a Lobster

1. Remove the red, cooked lobster from the pan. Place the lobster on its back and remove the legs and claws with a twisting action. Using the back of a wooden spoon, crack them open and carefully remove the meat. Remove the flesh, intact if possible, from the claws.

2. Turn the lobster over. Using a sharp knife, draw it through the head from the shoulder up towards the eye. Now cut along the centre of the body to the tail, splitting the lobster into two halves.

3. Remove and discard the white gills, the dark intestinal vein which goes along into the tail, and the small stomach sac, which lies in the head. Don't discard the green creamy liver in the head: it is a delicacy. Use it to make lobster sauce.

If you buy a female lobster, she may have an excellent red coral or roe, which can also be used in sauces.

4. Extract the white meat from the lobster and use as desired. To serve *au naturel*, cut the white meat into neat slices and place all the lobster meat in the cleaned shells or arrange attractively on a serving plate. Serve cold with mayonnaise or vinaigrette and a salad. Alternatively, place under a preheated moderate grill for a few minutes and serve warm with melted butter.

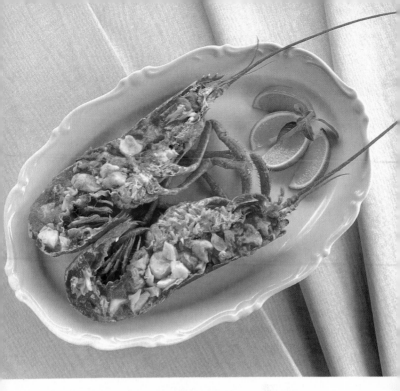

LOBSTER WITH TOMATO SAUCE

2 lobsters, about 500-750 g
  (1-1½ lb) each
25 g (1 oz) butter
1 tablespoon dry sherry
TOMATO SAUCE:
1 tablespoon sunflower oil
1 onion, finely chopped
1 carrot, finely chopped
2 cloves garlic, crushed
1 × 793 g (1 lb 12 oz)
  can tomatoes or 1 kg
  (2 lb) fresh tomatoes,
  skinned
1 teaspoon sugar
150 ml (¼ pint) dry red
  wine
salt and pepper
½ teaspoon chilli powder
½ teaspoon cayenne
  pepper
TO GARNISH:
lime wedges
basil sprigs

First make the tomato sauce. Heat the oil in a pan, add the onion and carrot and fry until golden. Add the garlic, tomatoes with their juice, sugar, wine, and salt and pepper to taste. Bring to the boil, stirring with a wooden spoon to break up the tomatoes, then simmer for 20 to 30 minutes, until thickened.

Rub through a sieve, or work in an electric blender or food processor, and return to the pan. Stir in the chilli powder and cayenne pepper.

Prepare the lobster as described opposite and slice the meat into pieces. Clean the shells and set aside.

Add the lobster meat to the warm tomato sauce and heat through. Stir in the butter and sherry. Return to the shells or place on a serving plate.

Garnish with lime wedges and basil to serve.

Serves 4 to 6

81

LOBSTER THERMIDOR

450 ml (¾ pint) milk
1 onion, cut into quarters
1 bay leaf
bouquet garni
150 ml (¼ pint) dry
  white wine
3 cooked lobsters, about
  500-750 g (1-1½ lb)
  each
125 g (4 oz) unsalted
  butter
50 g (2 oz) plain flour
2 teaspoons Dijon
  mustard
2 large egg yolks
142 ml (5 fl oz) single
  cream
2 teaspoons lemon juice
2 tablespoons finely
  chopped parsley
salt and pepper
TOPPING:
50 g (2 oz) fresh
  breadcrumbs
75 g (3 oz) Parmesan
  cheese, grated
TO GARNISH:
lemon or lime wedges
parsley sprigs

Pour the milk into a saucepan and add the onion, bay leaf and bouquet garni. Bring to the boil, then remove from the heat and leave to infuse for 30 minutes.

Place the wine in a small pan and boil for 3 minutes to reduce.

Prepare the lobsters as described on page 80. Cut the meat into 1 cm (½ inch) pieces and set aside. Sieve any coral and set aside. Clean the shells and set aside.

Melt half the butter in a frying pan, add the lobster meat and cook gently, stirring, for 2 minutes. Remove from the heat.

Melt the remaining butter in another pan, stir in the flour and cook for 1 minute. Remove from the heat.

Strain the infused milk, then gradually beat into the roux. Add the reduced wine, bring gently to the boil, then simmer for 4 minutes. Leave to cool then stir in the mustard, egg yolks, coral, if present, cream, lemon juice, parsley, and salt and pepper to taste. Spoon a little of this sauce into the bottom of each lobster shell.

Add the lobster meat to the remaining sauce and stir gently. Spoon into the shells and sprinkle with the breadcrumbs and cheese.

Place on a baking sheet and cook in a preheated moderately hot oven, 200°C (400°F), Gas Mark 6, for 7 to 10 minutes, until golden brown. Garnish with lemon or lime wedges and parsley. Serve immediately.
Serves 6

SAUCES AND ACCOMPANIMENTS

Many fish dishes are enhanced by accompanying sauces and savoury butters. Here you will find plenty of ideas to choose from. These accompaniments are quick and easy to prepare – and well worth the effort. The butters and cold sauces can be prepared well ahead and stored in the refrigerator until required.

GOOSEBERRY SAUCE

500 g (1 lb) gooseberries
2 tablespoons water
25 g (1 oz) butter
1 tablespoon demerara sugar
1 egg
salt and white pepper

Place the gooseberries and water in a pan, bring to the boil, then simmer for 20 minutes. Stir in the butter and sugar.

Whisk the egg until pale and fluffy, using an electric blender or beater. Carefully pour the hot gooseberries onto the egg, while the motor is running, to form an emulsion. Season with salt and pepper. Serve hot or cold with mackerel or herring.
Makes 350 ml (12 fl oz)

HAMPAGNE SAUCE

s is a delicious sauce, worth making for a special occasion. It
aditionally served with shellfish, such as lobster, scallops and
yfish.

25 g (1 oz) unsalted
  butter
3 shallots, finely chopped
300 ml (½ pint)
  champagne
284 ml (10 fl oz) single
  cream
salt and pepper
2 tablespoons finely
  chopped chervil
  (optional)
2 tablespoons finely
  chopped tarragon
  (optional)
50 g (2 oz) mushrooms,
  finely sliced (optional)

Melt the butter in a pan, stir in the
shallots and fry for 5 minutes, until
softened.

Pour in the champagne, bring to
the boil, and boil gently for about
15 minutes, until reduced by half.
Remove from the heat and cool
slightly. Stir in the cream, add salt
and pepper to taste, return to the heat
and heat gently until thick enough to
coat the back of a spoon. Stir in the
herbs and mushrooms, if using.

Serve hot, with shellfish or
poached salmon.

Makes 350 ml (12 fl oz)

WHITE SAUCE

25 g (1 oz) butter
25 g (1 oz) plain flour
300 ml (½ pint) milk
salt and pepper

Melt the butter in a pan, stir in the flour and cook, stirring, for 1 min Remove from the heat and gradual beat in the milk, and salt and pepper to taste. Return to the heat, bring to the boil and cook for 2 minutes, stirring constantly.

Serve hot with plaice, haddock, cod.

Makes 300 ml (½ pint)

VARIATIONS:

Parsley Sauce: Stir 50 g (2 oz) chopped parsley into the finished sauce.

Cheese Sauce: Stir 75 g (3 oz) grated Cheddar cheese and 1 teaspoon dry mustard into the finished sauce.

Mushroom Sauce: Sauté 50 g (2 oz) sliced mushrooms in 15 g (½ oz) butter with 1 teaspoon lemon juice for 5 minutes. Stir into the finished sauce.

Onion Sauce: Sauté 1 finely chopped onion in the butter for 7 minutes, before stirring in the flour.

Caper Sauce: Stir 1 tablespoon finely chopped capers and 1 teaspoon lemon juice into the finished sauce.

Prawn Sauce: Stir 75 g (3 oz) peeled prawns and ½ teaspoon cayenne pepper into the finished sauce.

BÉCHAMEL SAUCE

300 ml (½ pint) milk
1 small onion, quartered
1 bay leaf
2 thyme sprigs
1 parsley sprig
pinch of grated nutmeg
salt and pepper
25 g (1 oz) butter
25 g (1 oz) plain flour

Pour the milk into a saucepan and add the onion, herbs, nutmeg, and salt and pepper to taste. Bring slowly to the boil, remove from the heat at once, cover and leave to infuse for 30 minutes to 1 hour, then strain.

Melt the butter in a pan, stir in the flour and cook, stirring, for 1 minute. Remove from the heat and gradually stir in the strained milk. Return to the heat, bring to the boil and cook for 2 minutes, stirring constantly. Check the seasoning.

Makes 300 ml (½ pint)

MUSTARD SAUCE

1 large egg yolk
2 tablespoons Dijon
    mustard
½ teaspoon sugar
1 tablespoon wine vinegar
6 tablespoons oil
salt and pepper
1 tablespoon chopped dill

Beat the egg yolk with the mustard and sugar until smooth. Stir in the vinegar. Gradually beat in the oil and add salt and pepper to taste. Stir in the dill. Serve cold.
Makes 120 ml (4 fl oz)

FRESH HERB SAUCE

2 packets of watercress
1 bunch of parsley
2 tarragon sprigs
4 chervil sprigs
2 tablespoons lemon juice
4 tablespoons oil
350 g (12 oz) fromage
    blanc

Finely chop the watercress and herbs and place in a bowl. Gradually stir in the lemon juice and oil, then the fromage blanc. Season with salt and pepper to taste.
  Serve warm, heated very gently, or cold, with scallops and trout fillets.
Makes 450 ml (¾ pint)

SPICY GOOSEBERRY SAUCE

500 g (1 lb) gooseberries
1 clove garlic, crushed
1 teaspoon salt
2 teaspoons dry mustard
150 ml (¼ pint) white
    wine vinegar
175 g (6 oz) demerara
    sugar
50 g (2 oz) sultanas
150 ml (¼ pint) water

Place all the ingredients in a saucepan, bring to the boil, stirring, then simmer for 40 minutes, stirring occasionally. Cool slightly, then place in an electric blender or food processor and work until smooth; rub through a sieve to remove the pips.
  Serve hot or cold. Delicious with baked herring and mackerel.
Makes 350 ml (12 fl oz)

TARTARE SAUCE

4 teaspoons capers
3 cocktail gherkins
a few chives
150 ml (¼ pint)
   mayonnaise
2 tablespoons yogurt

Chop the capers, gherkins and chives.
Mix all the ingredients together.
Serve cold.
Makes 200 ml (⅓ pint)

HORSERADISH AND DILL SAUCE

2 tablespoons grated
   horseradish
2 tablespoons lemon juice
1 small dessert apple,
   peeled, cored and grated
142 ml (5 fl oz) soured
   cream
1 tablespoon chopped dill
salt and pepper

Stir the horseradish, lemon juice and
apple into the soured cream.
   Add the dill, and salt and pepper to
taste.
   Serve hot or cold. To serve hot,
heat through very gently; do not
allow to boil.
Makes 150 ml (¼ pint)

TOMATO SAUCE

1 tablespoon oil
50 g (2 oz) mushrooms,
   finely chopped
1 onion, finely chopped
1 clove garlic, crushed
1 × 397 g (14 oz) can
   chopped tomatoes
6 tablespoons red wine
1 teaspoon tomato purée
1 bay leaf
salt and pepper

Heat the oil in a pan, add the
mushrooms and onion and sauté for
3 minutes, until softened.
   Add the remaining ingredients,
with salt and pepper to taste, bring to
the boil, then simmer for 20 to
30 minutes, stirring occasionally,
until the desired consistency. Remove
the bay leaf.
Makes about 300 ml (½ pint)

HOLLANDAISE SAUCE

3 tablespoons white wine
   vinegar
1 tablespoon water
6 peppercorns
1 bay leaf
3 egg yolks
175 g (6 oz) unsalted
   butter, cut into cubes
salt and white pepper
1 teaspoon lemon juice
   (optional)

Place the vinegar, water, peppercorns and bay leaf in a pan, bring to the boil and boil until reduced to approximately 1 tablespoon liquid.

Place the egg yolks and 15 g (½ oz) of the butter in a heatproof bowl and cream until soft. Strain in the vinegar.

Place the bowl over a pan two-thirds filled with boiling water. Beat in the cubes of butter one at a time, mixing thoroughly until the sauce is creamy and shiny. If it refuses to thicken, turn the heat up a little; if it shows signs of thickening too soon or curdling, remove it from the pan and place in a bowl of cold water, stirring all the time. Stir in salt and pepper and lemon juice, if using.

Serve warm. Ideal with poached salmon, trout and baked sea bass.
Makes 300 ml (½ pint)

PIQUANT TOMATO SAUCE

1 kg (2 lb) tomatoes,
  roughly chopped
4 shallots, chopped
½ carrot, grated
4 tablespoons orange juice
1 teaspoon grated orange
  rind
1 teaspoon salt
1½ tablespoons sugar
1 teaspoon paprika

Place all the ingredients in a saucepan, bring to the boil, then simmer for 15 minutes. Rub through a fine sieve to form a smooth sauce.

Serve hot or cold. Excellent served with scallops or Scallop and Prawn Brochettes (see page 58).
Makes 600 ml (1 pint)

EASY HOLLANDAISE SAUCE

If you have problems with traditional Hollandaise Sauce, this is an easier version, which tastes just as good.

15 g (½ oz) butter
15 g (½ oz) plain flour
150 ml (¼ pint) hot
  water (not boiling)
2 egg yolks
125 g (4 oz) butter, cut
  into cubes
1 tablespoon lemon juice
salt and white pepper

Melt the butter in a pan, stir in the flour and cook, stirring, for 1 minute. Remove from the heat and gradually beat in the water. Return to the heat and gradually whisk in the egg yolks. Heat gently, whisking constantly, until the mixture begins to thicken. Remove from the heat and gently beat in the butter, one cube at a time. Stir in the lemon juice, and salt and pepper to taste.
Makes 300 ml (½ pint)

SAVOURY BUTTERS

These are excellent accompaniments to serve either melted or chilled, with fish.

Anchovy Butter

6 anchovy fillets
125 g (4 oz) unsalted
  butter, softened
1 teaspoon anchovy
  essence

Rinse the anchovies in cold water; dr
thoroughly. Chop finely, then rub
through a sieve. Beat into the butter
with the anchovy essence.
  Serve with grilled fish and
herrings.

Tarragon Butter

50 g (2 oz) tarragon
125 g (4 oz) unsalted
  butter, softened

Finely chop the tarragon and beat into
the butter. Serve on top of a hot
turbot steak.

Pear Butter

1 × 213 g (7½ oz) can
  pear halves in natural
  juice, drained
125 g (4 oz) unsalted
  butter, softened
pepper

Place the pears in an electric blender
or food processor and work until
smooth. Beat in the butter and season
with pepper to taste.
  Serve on rye bread with smoked
salmon.

Maître d'Hôtel Butter

1 tablespoon finely
  chopped parsley
1 teaspoon grated lemon
  rind
1 tablespoon lemon juice
125 g (4 oz) unsalted
  butter, softened
salt and pepper

Beat all the ingredients together,
seasoning with salt and pepper to
taste.
  Serve with grilled fish, eg skate
wings.

INDEX